CZECHOSLOVAK FAIRY TALES

WITH ILLUSTRATIONS AND DECORATIONS
BY
JAN MATULKA

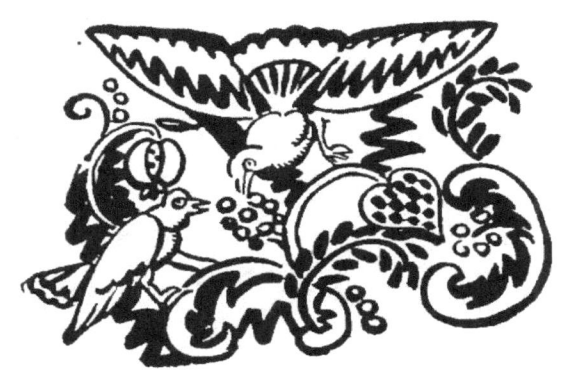

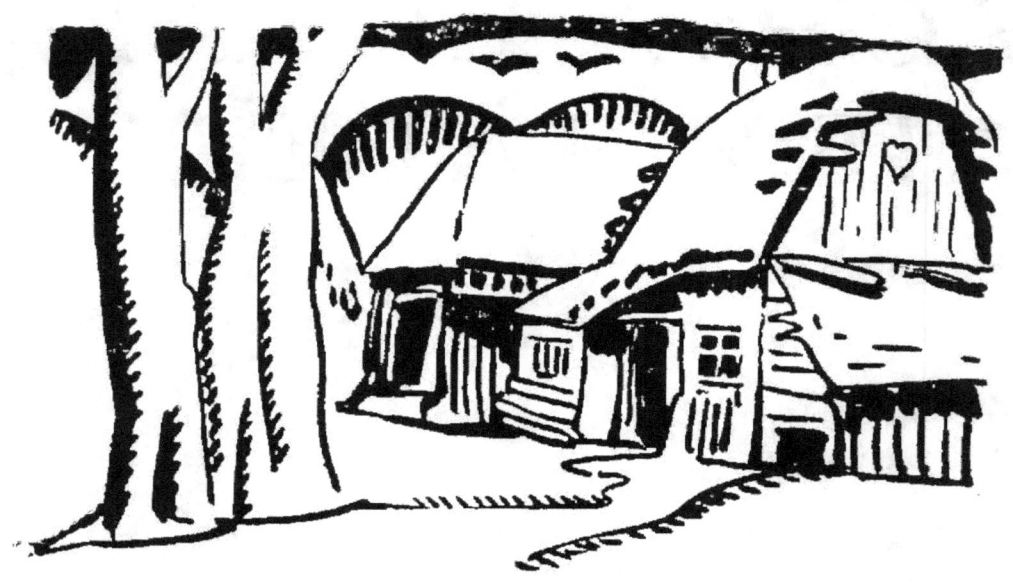

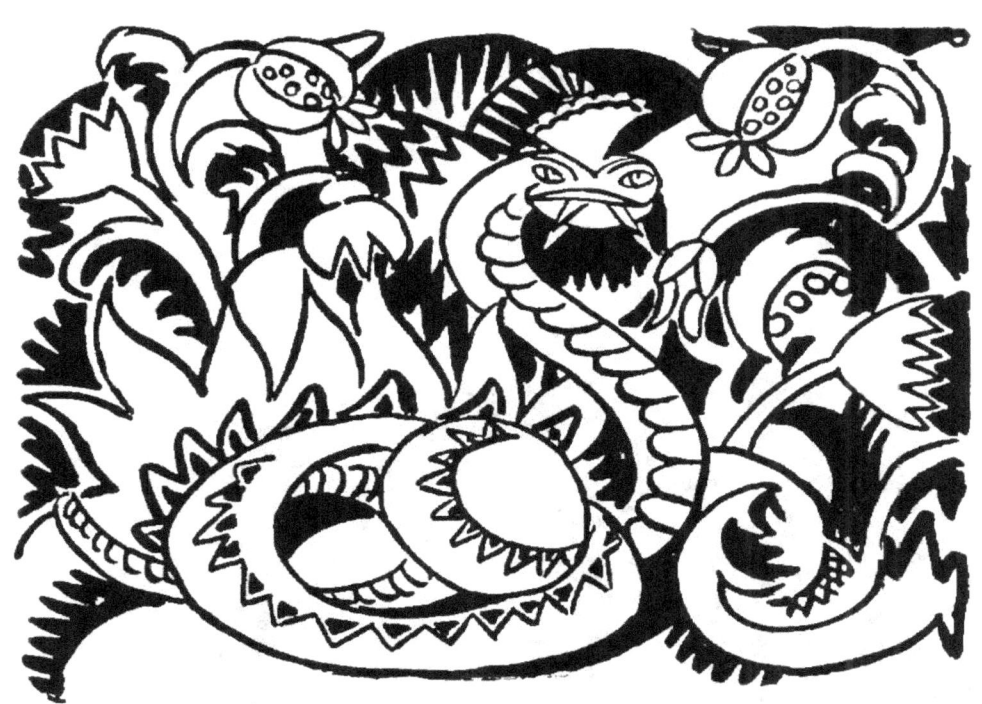

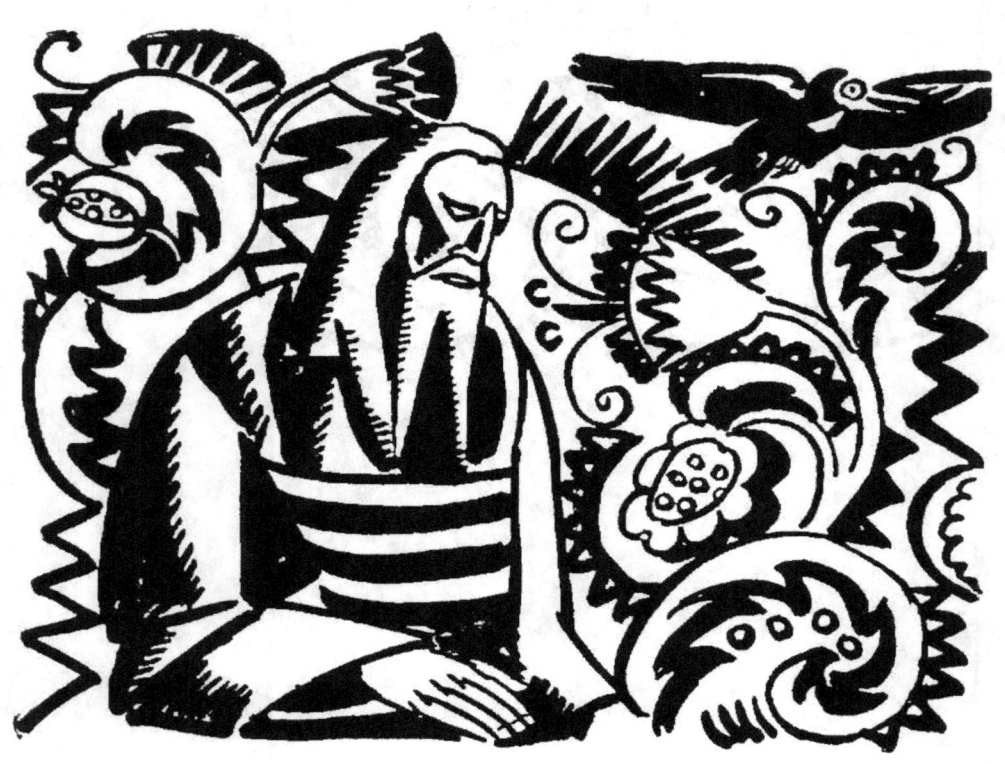

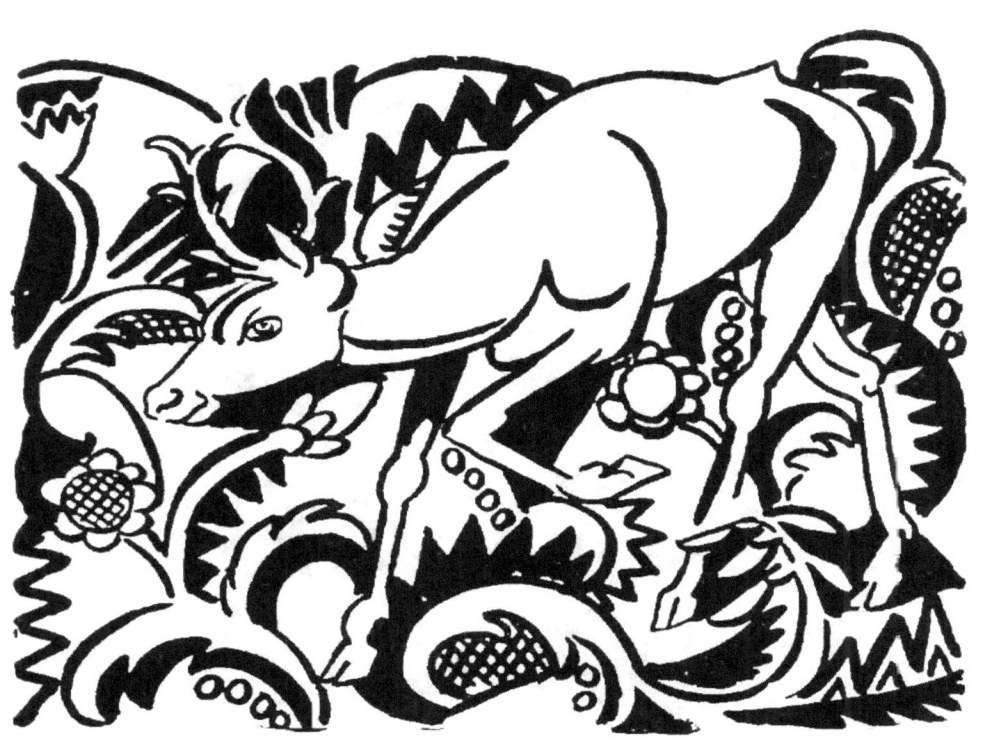

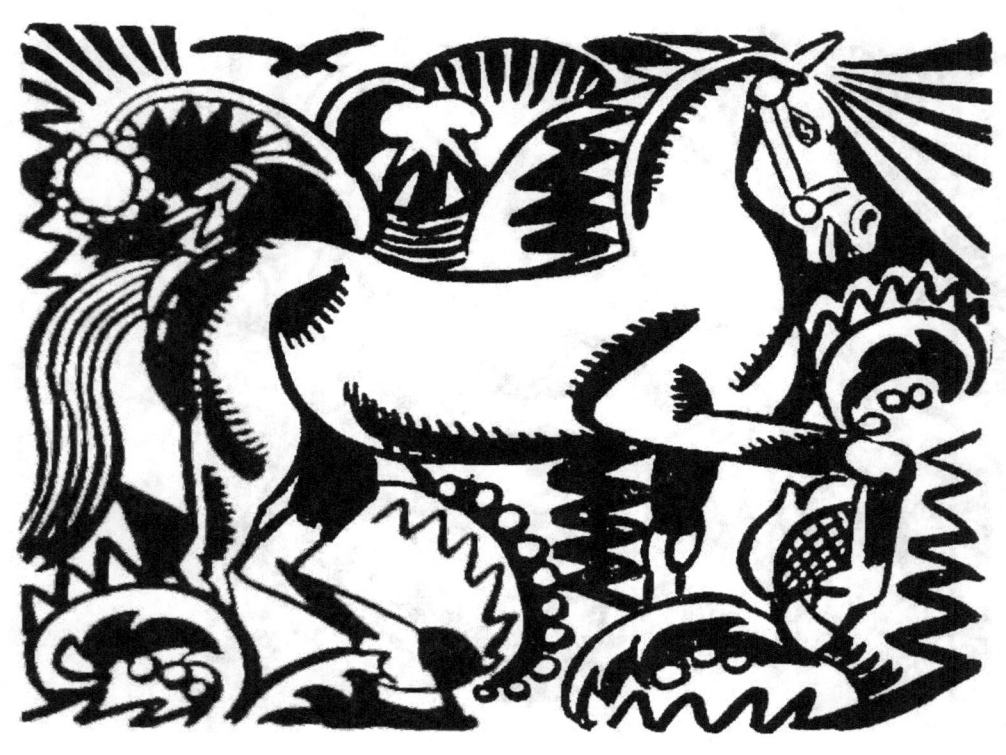

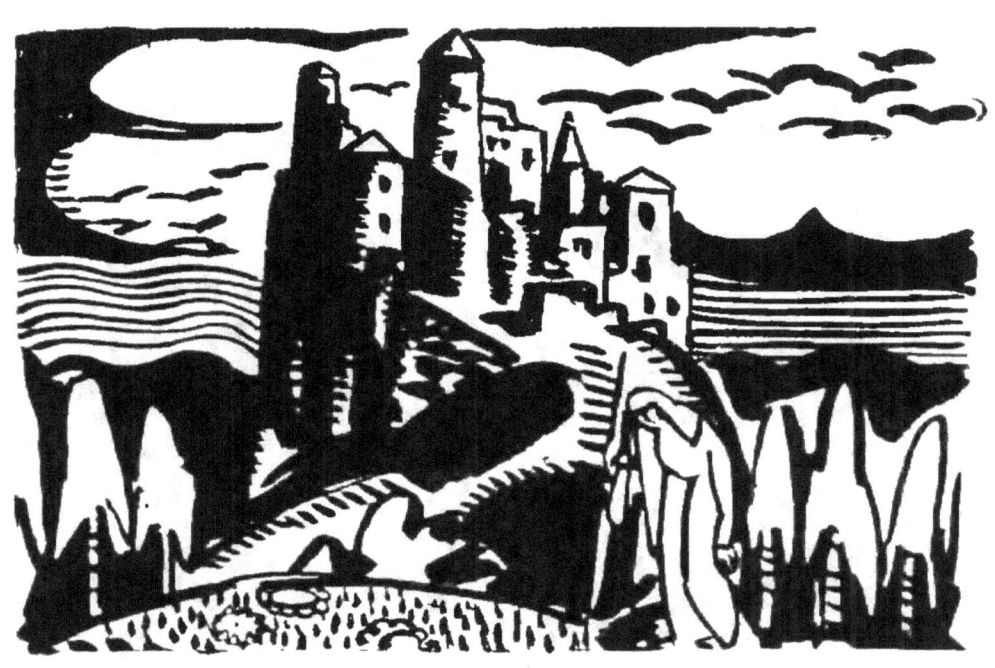

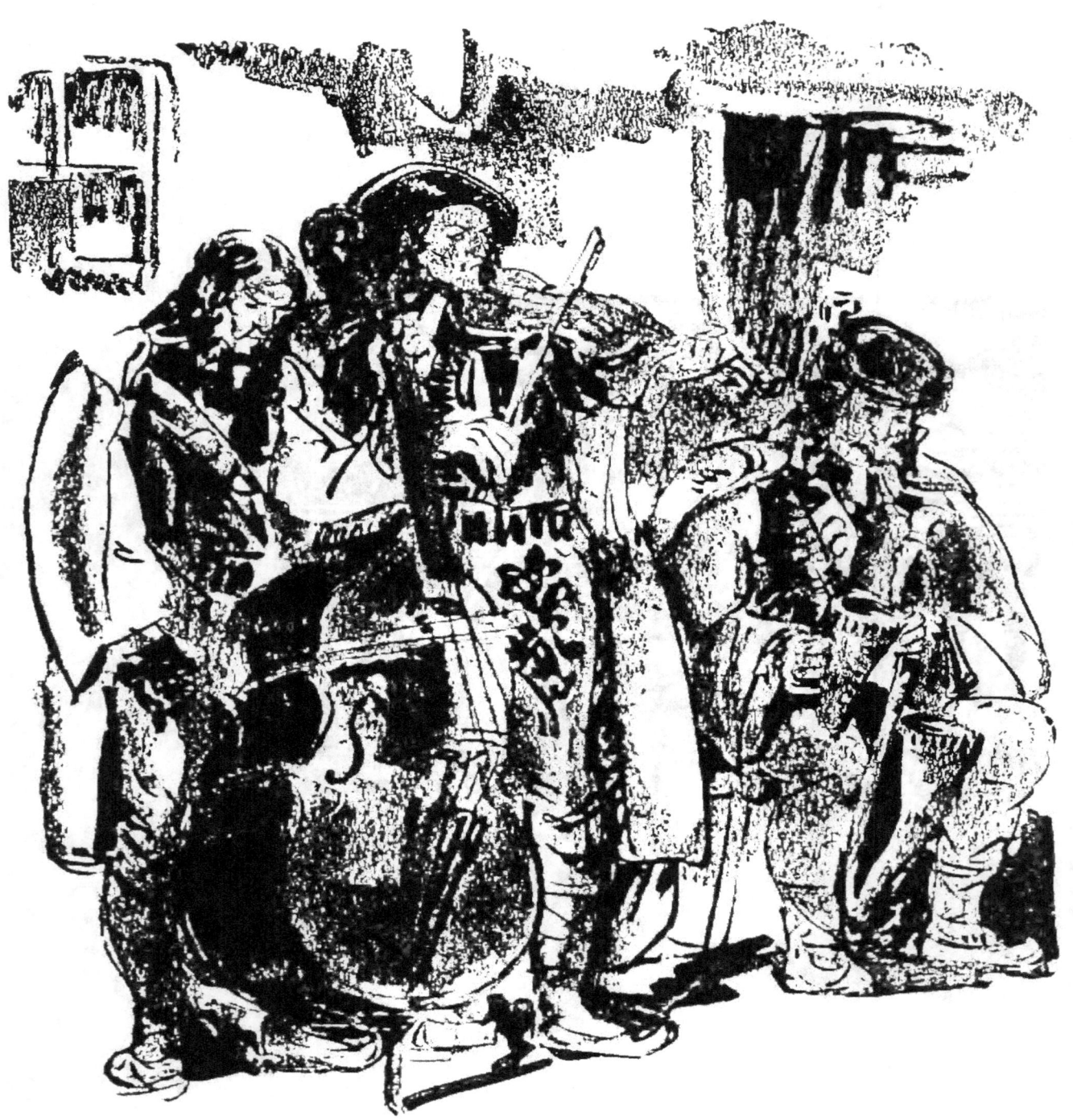

Music Played

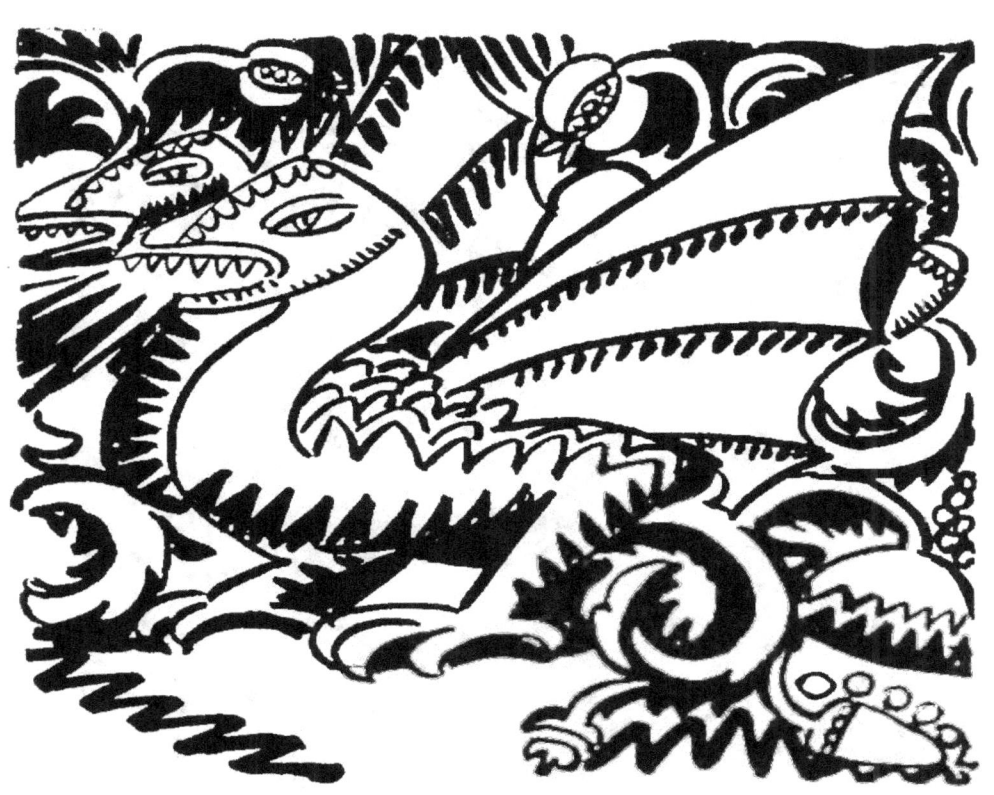

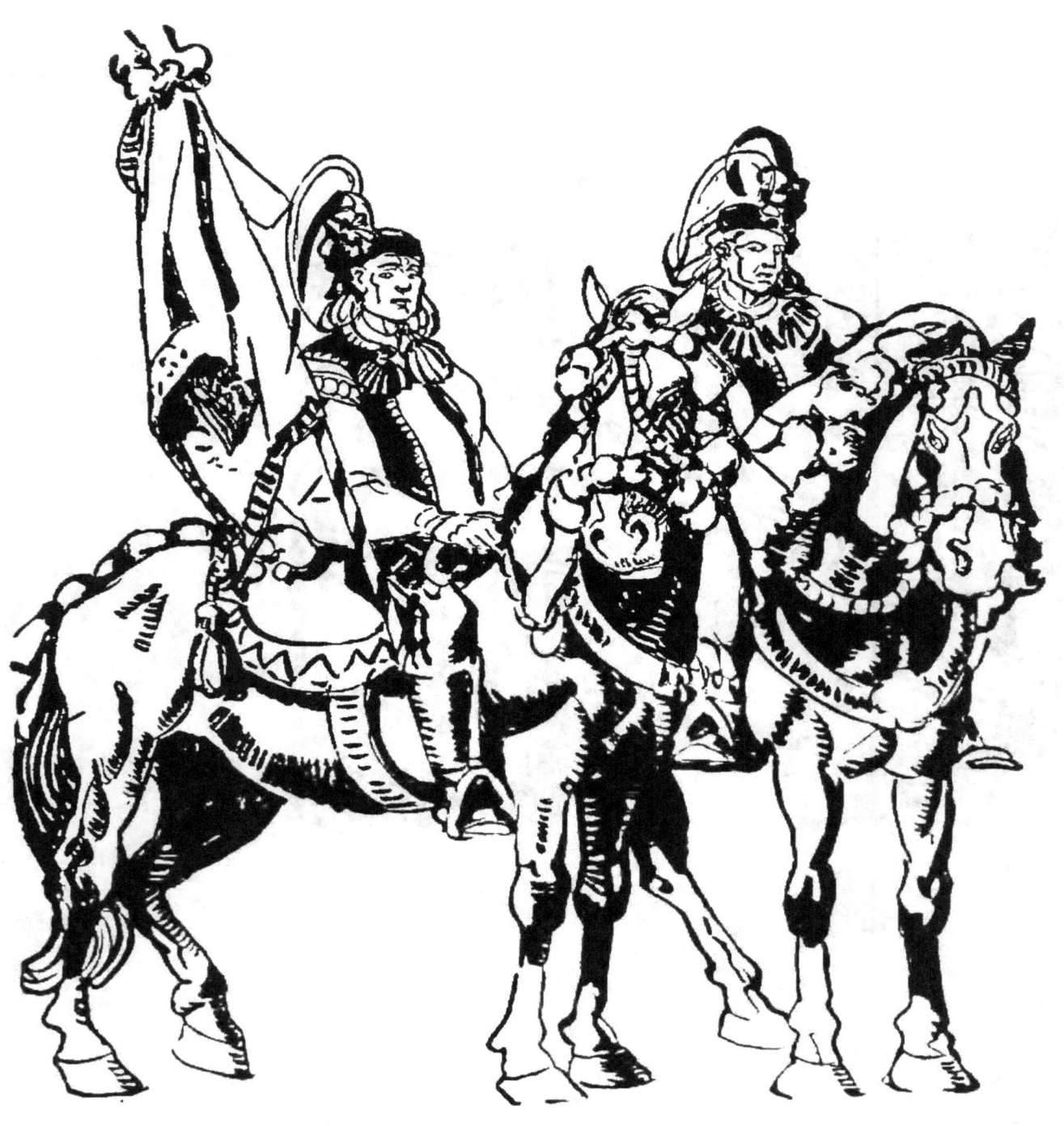

When the Boys Had Grown into Handsome Youths

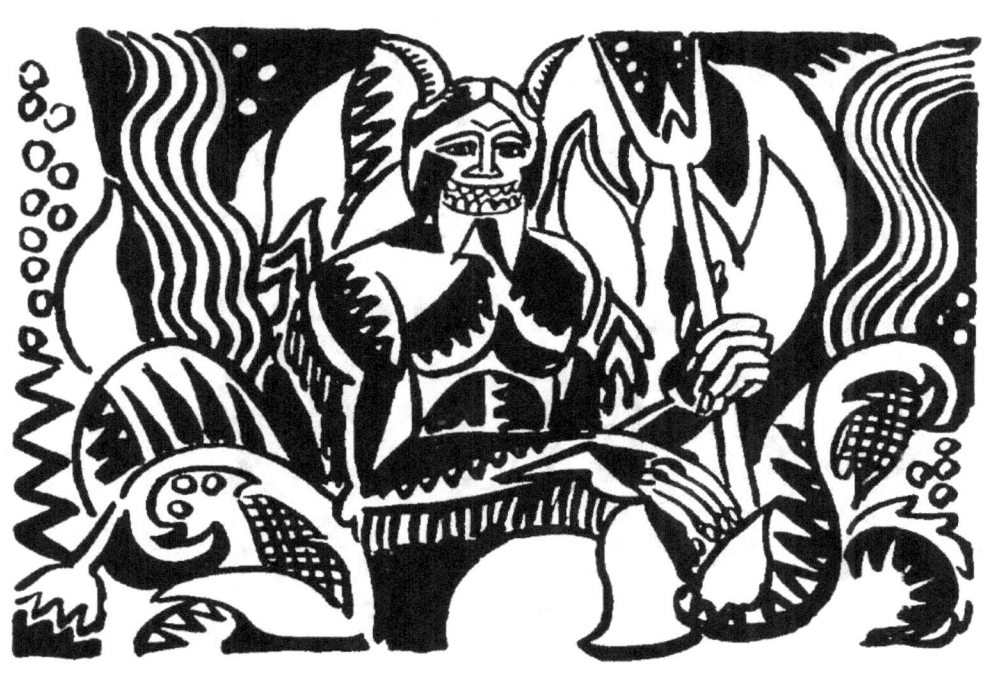

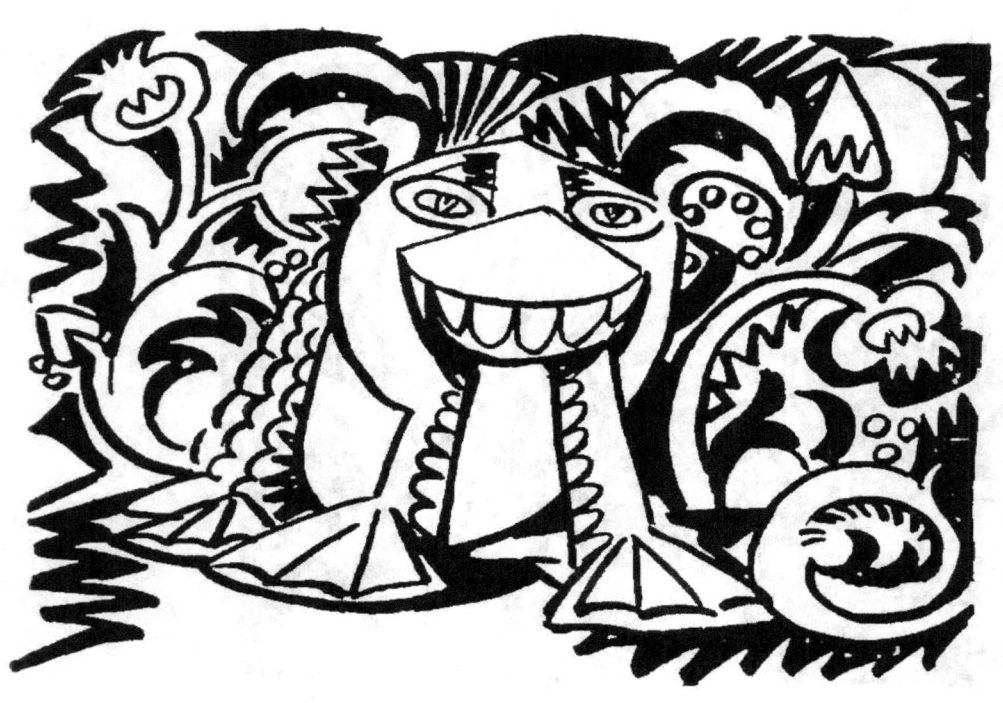

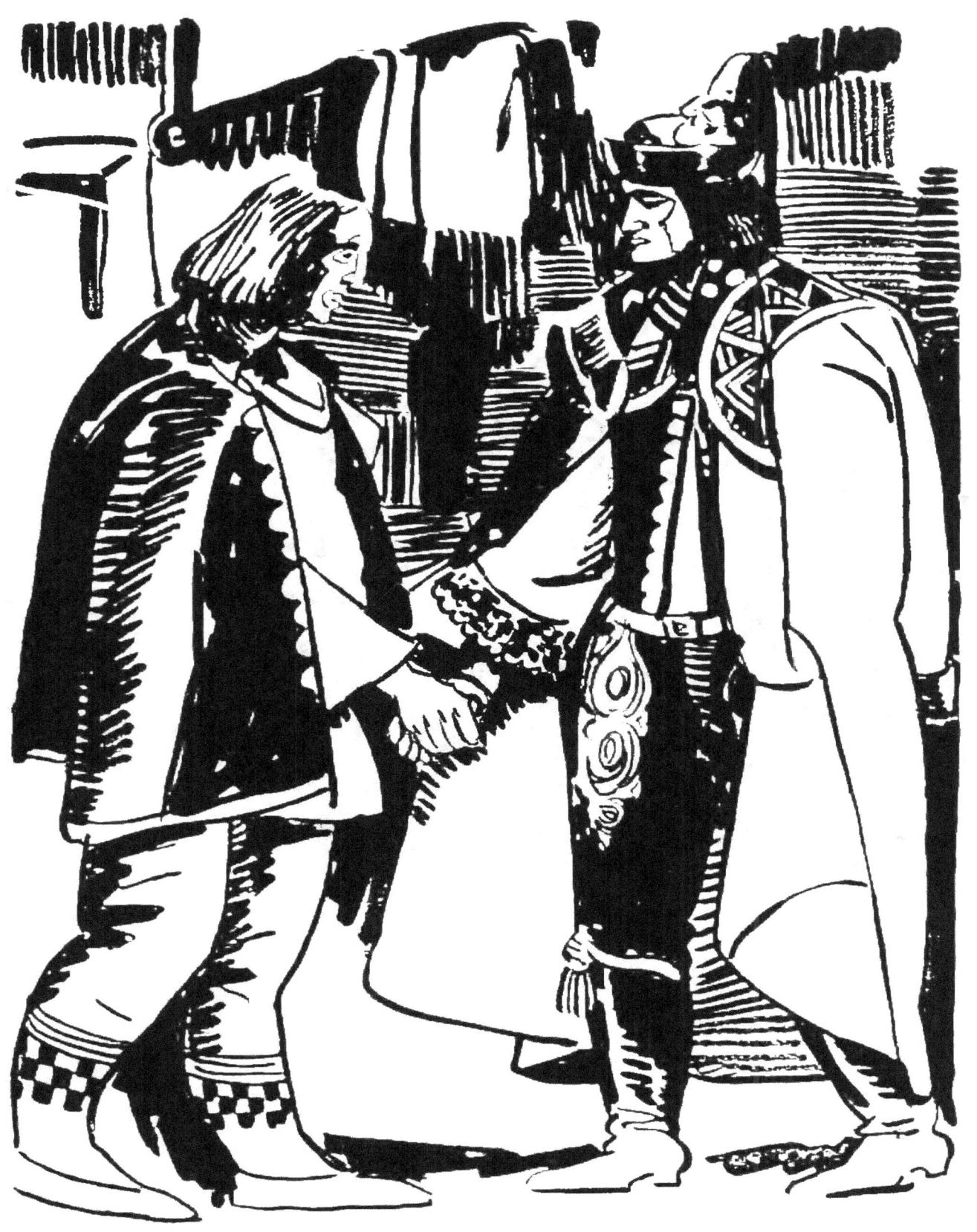

Kubik Greeting His Old Father

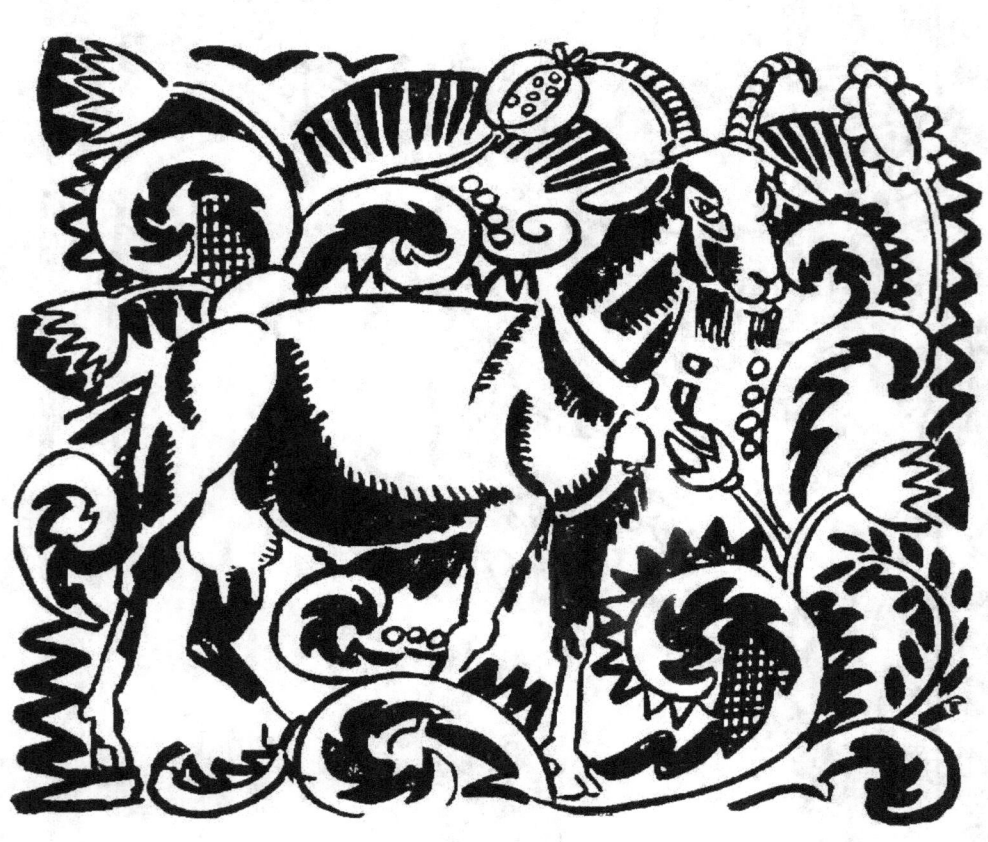

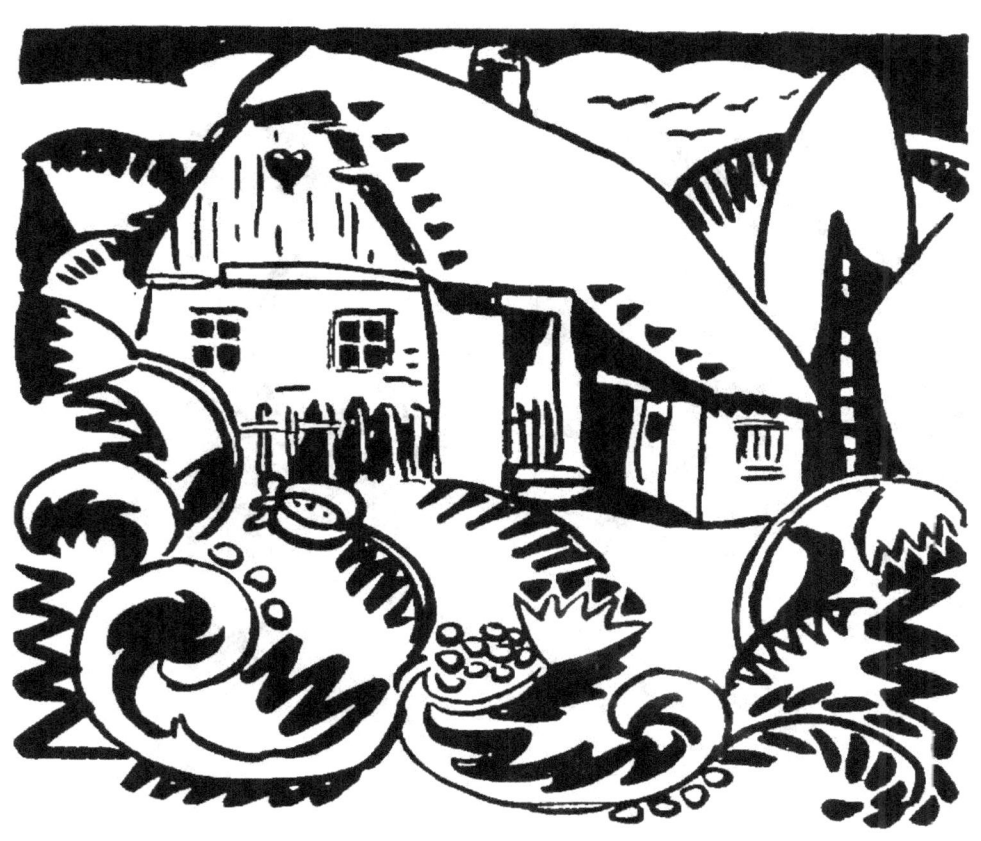

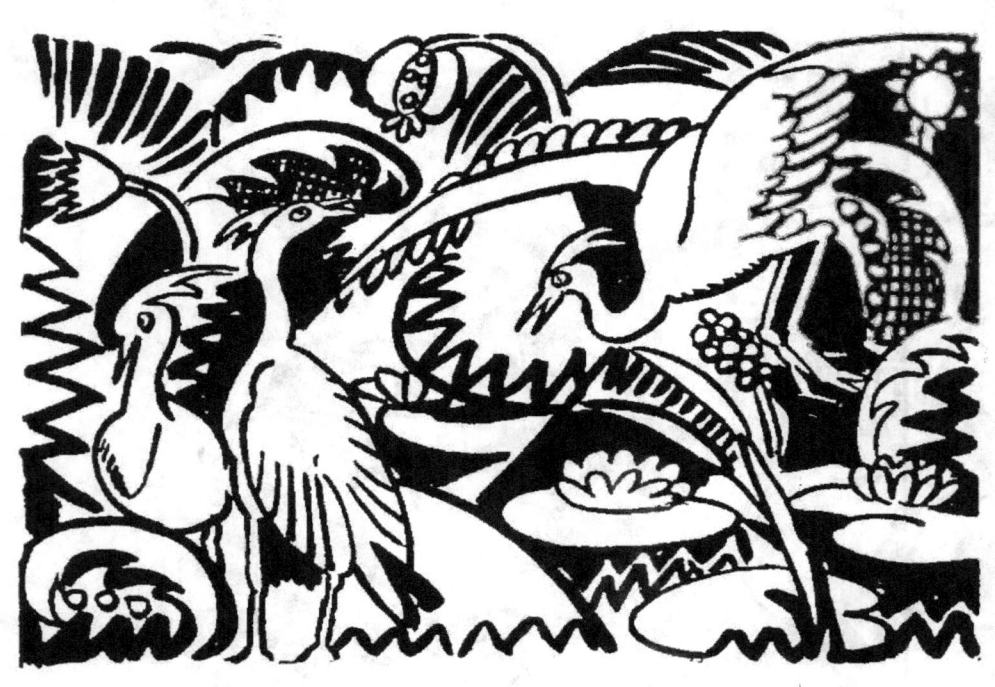

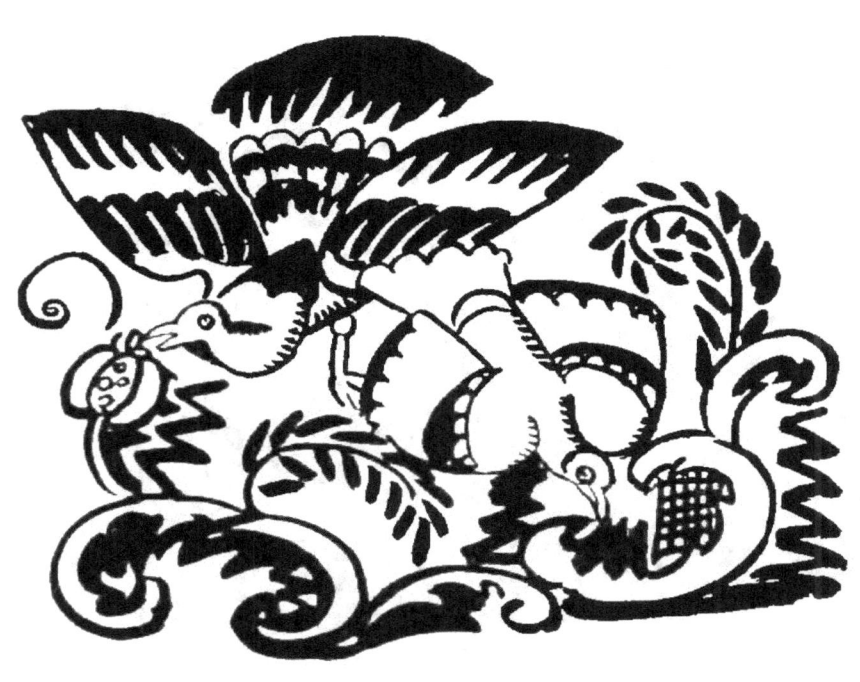

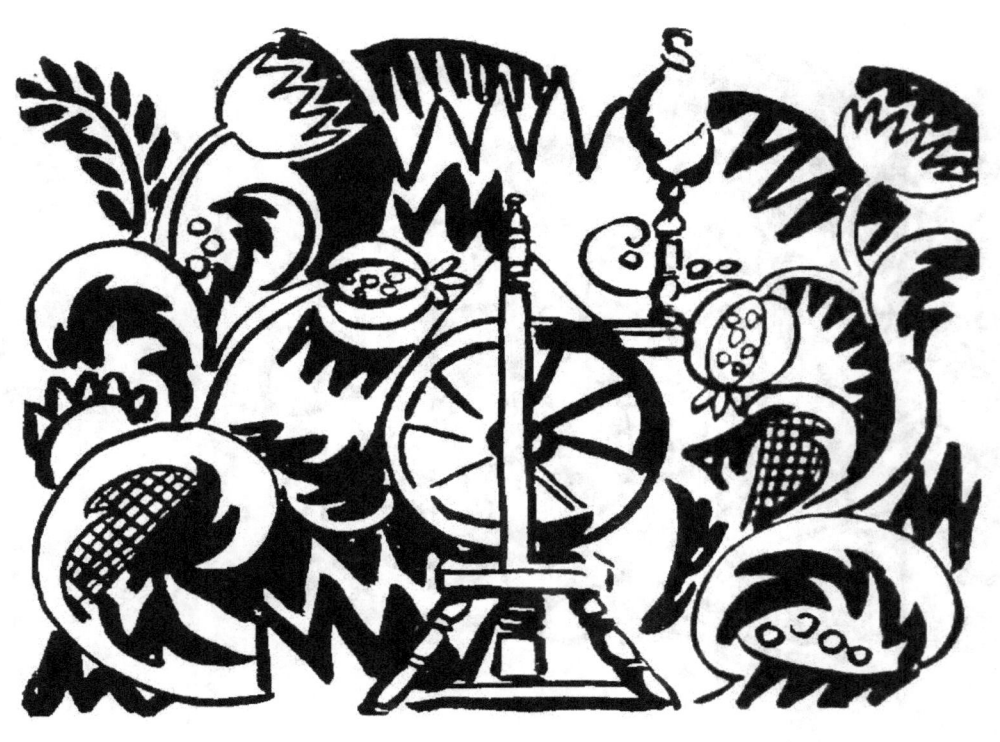

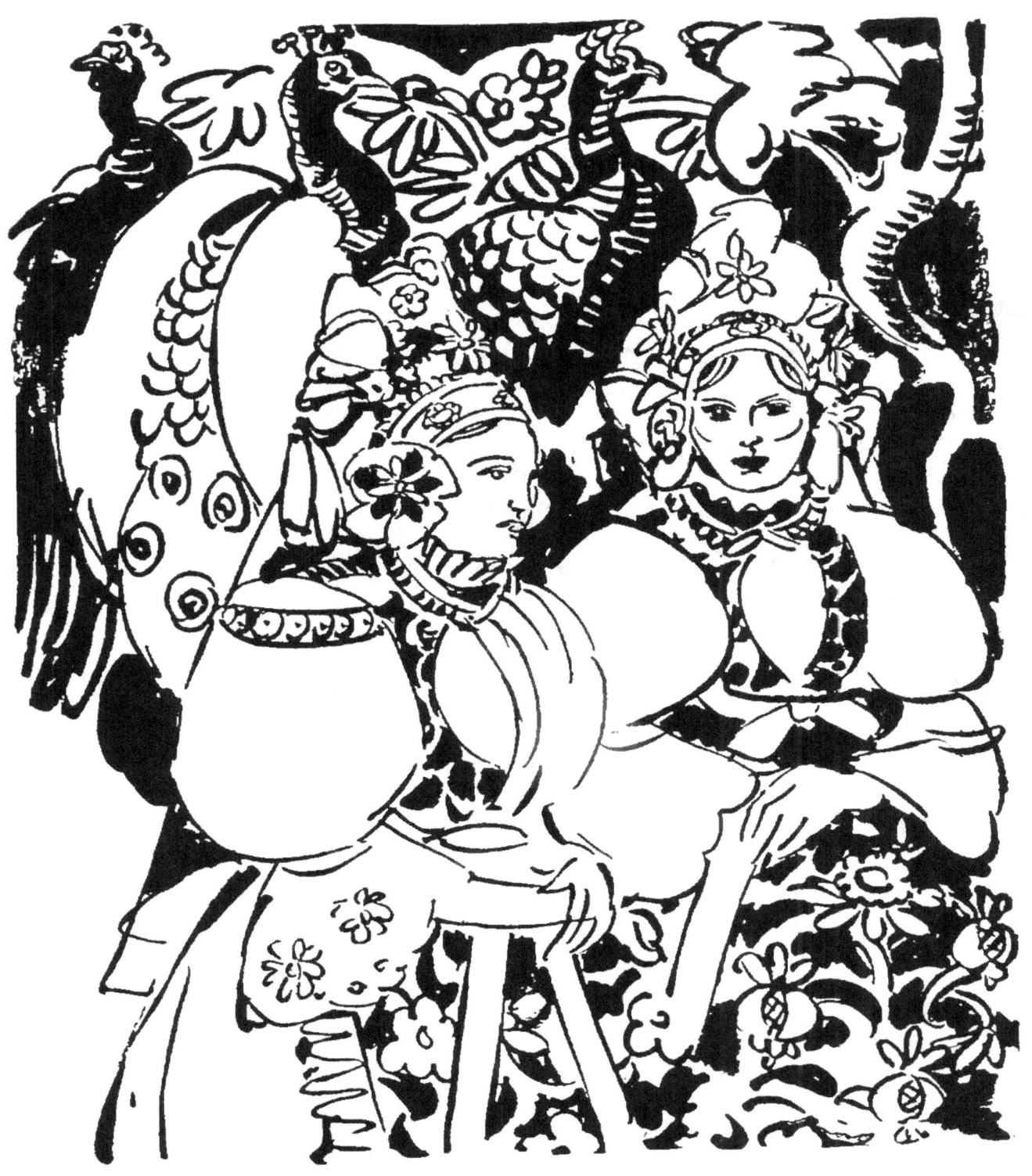

Alike in Feature but Utterly Different in Disposition

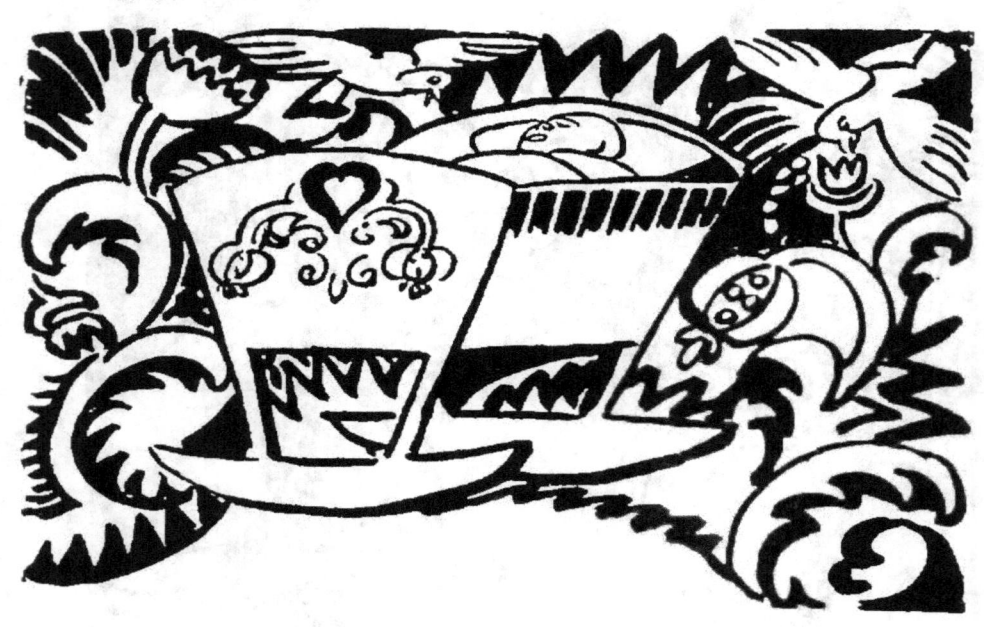

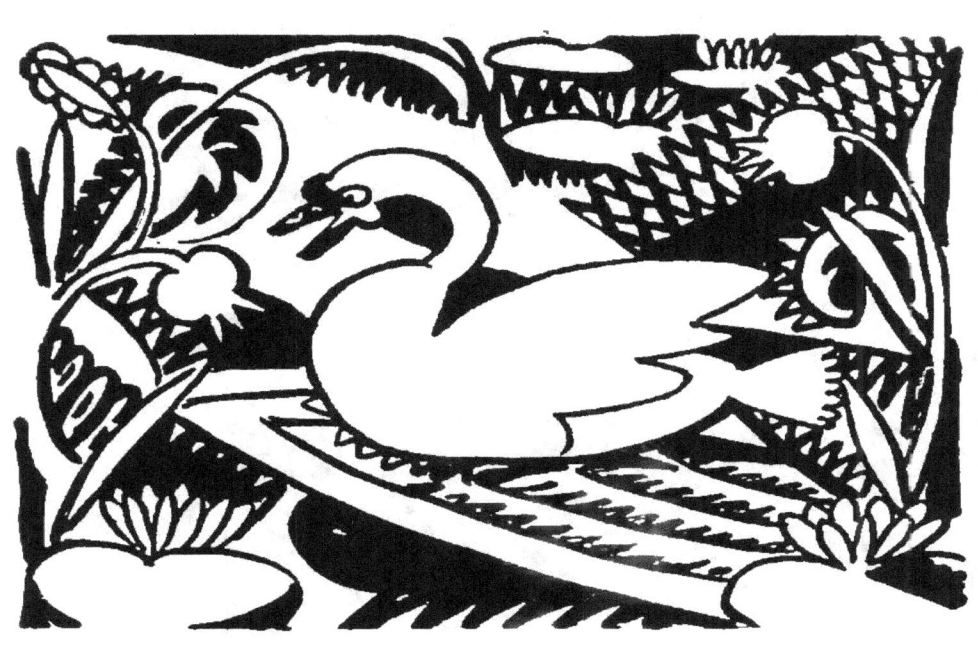

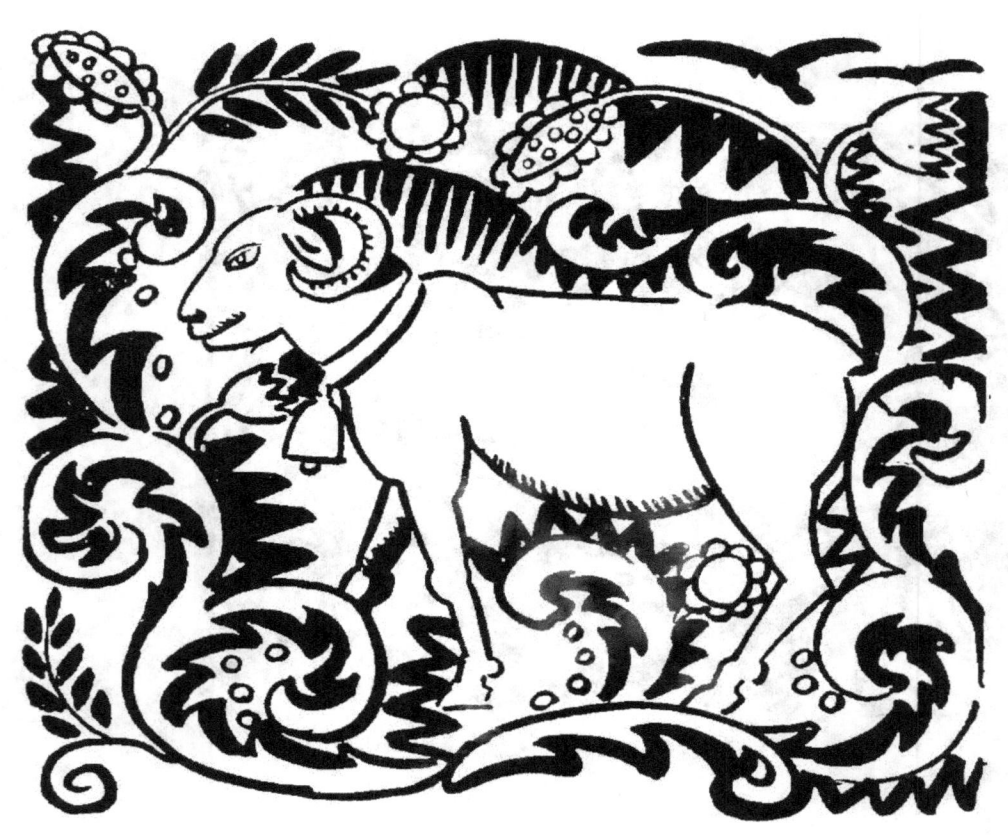

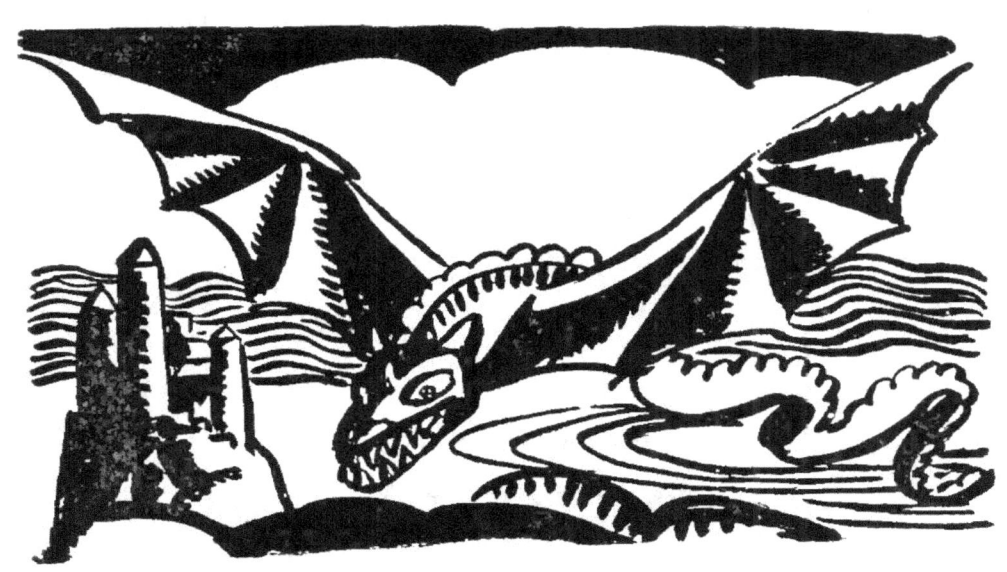

THE SHOEMAKER'S APRON

A Second Book of Czechoslovak Fairy Tales and Folk Tales

WITH ILLUSTRATIONS
AND DECORATIONS BY
JAN MATULKA

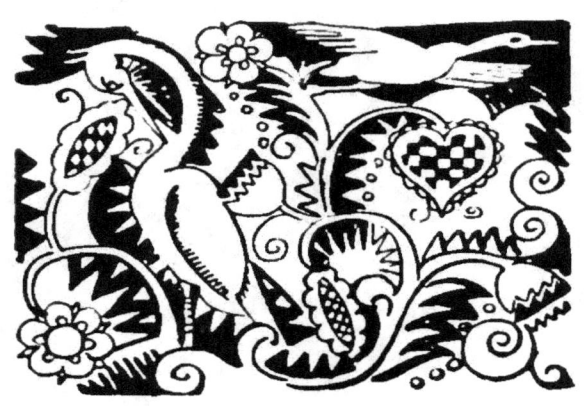

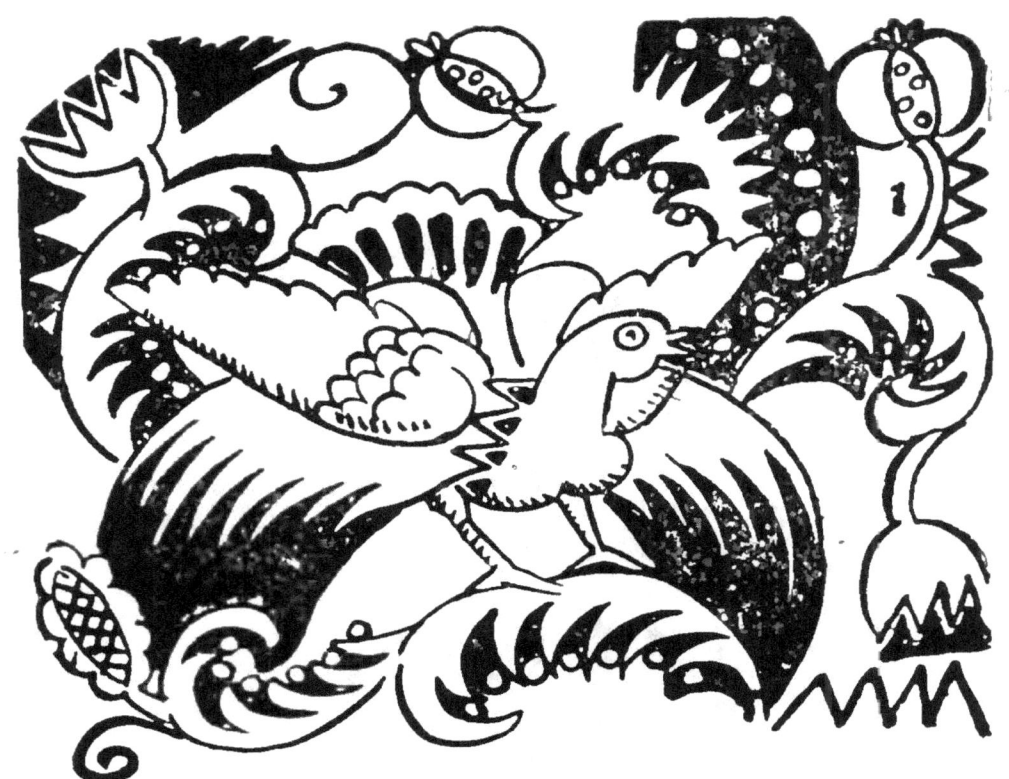

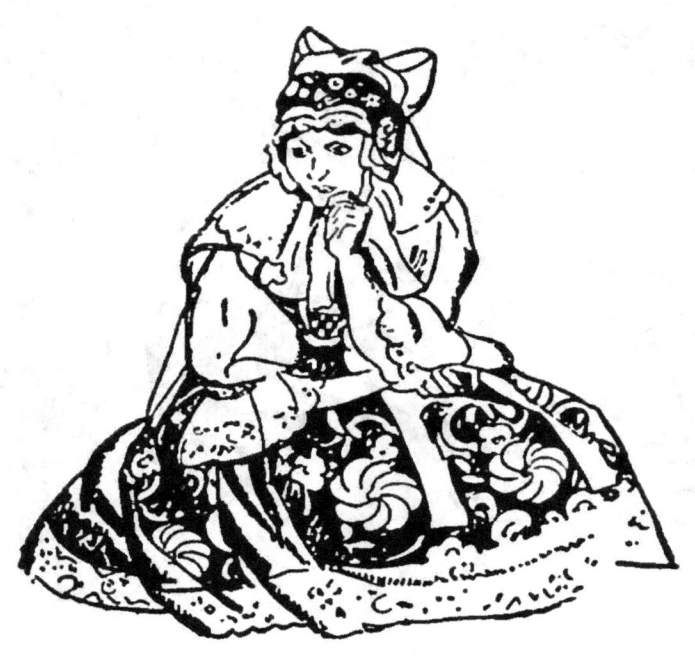

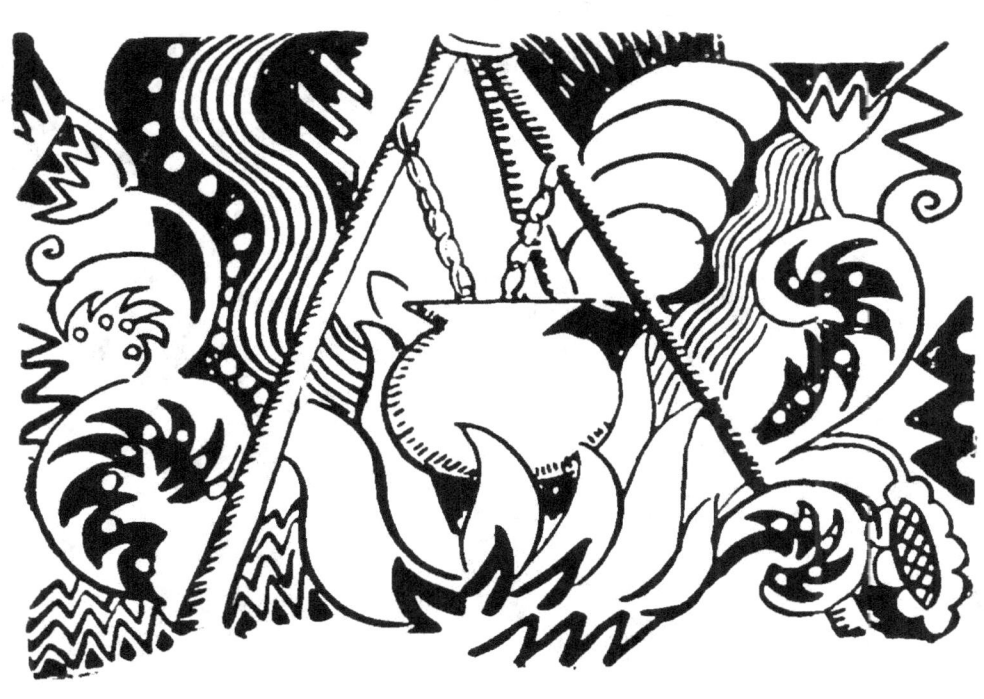

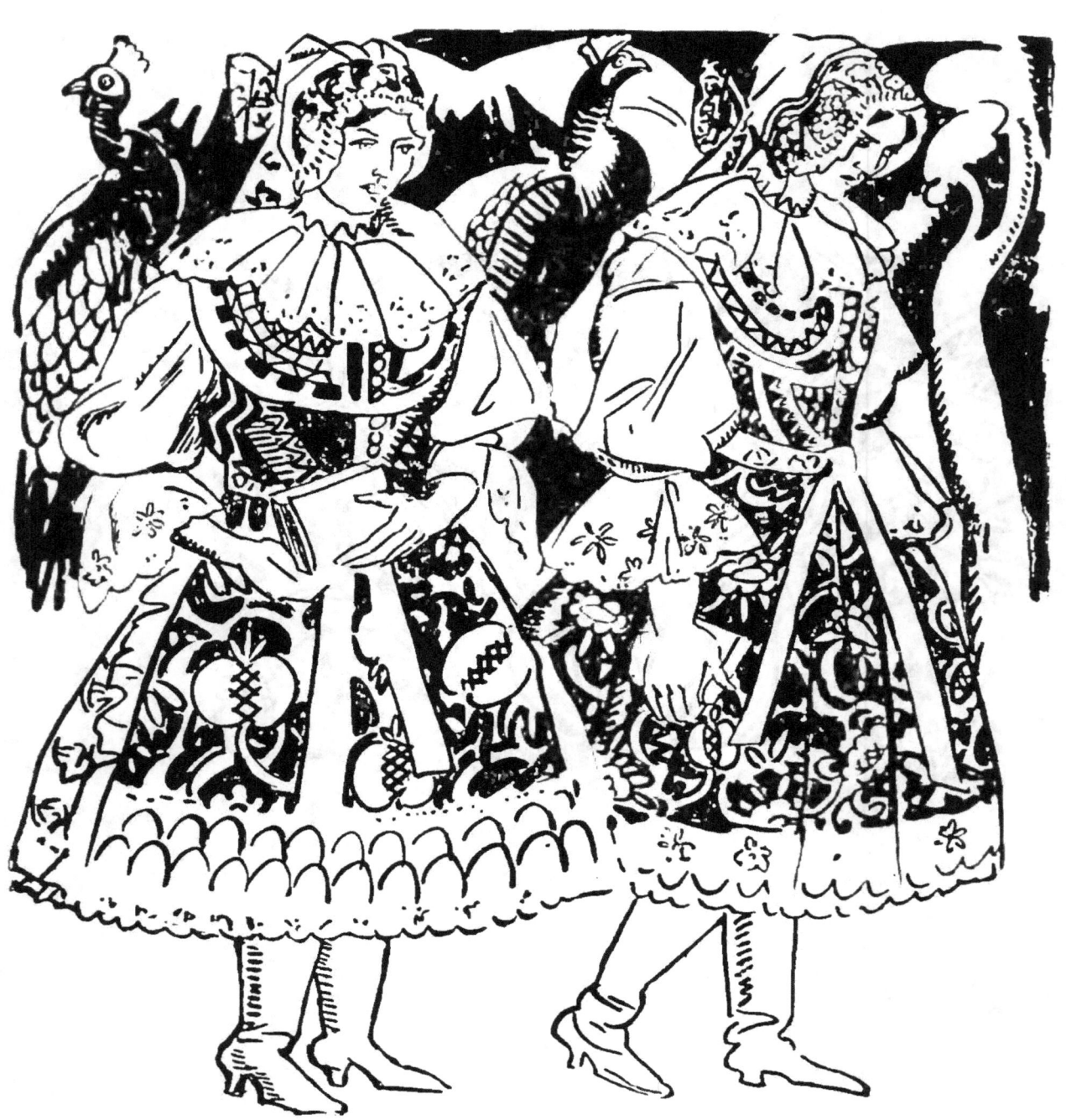

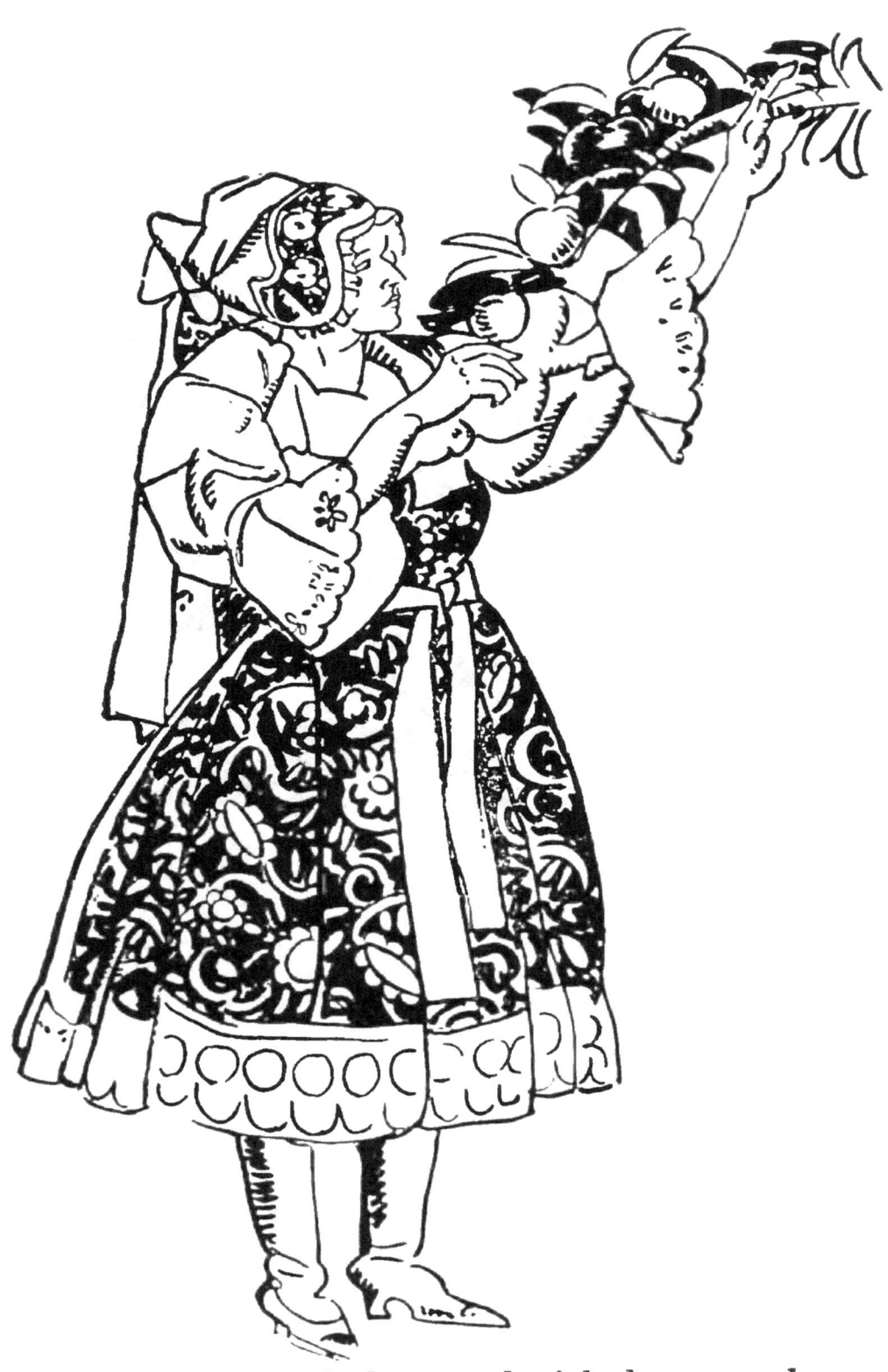

Marushka reached up and picked one apple

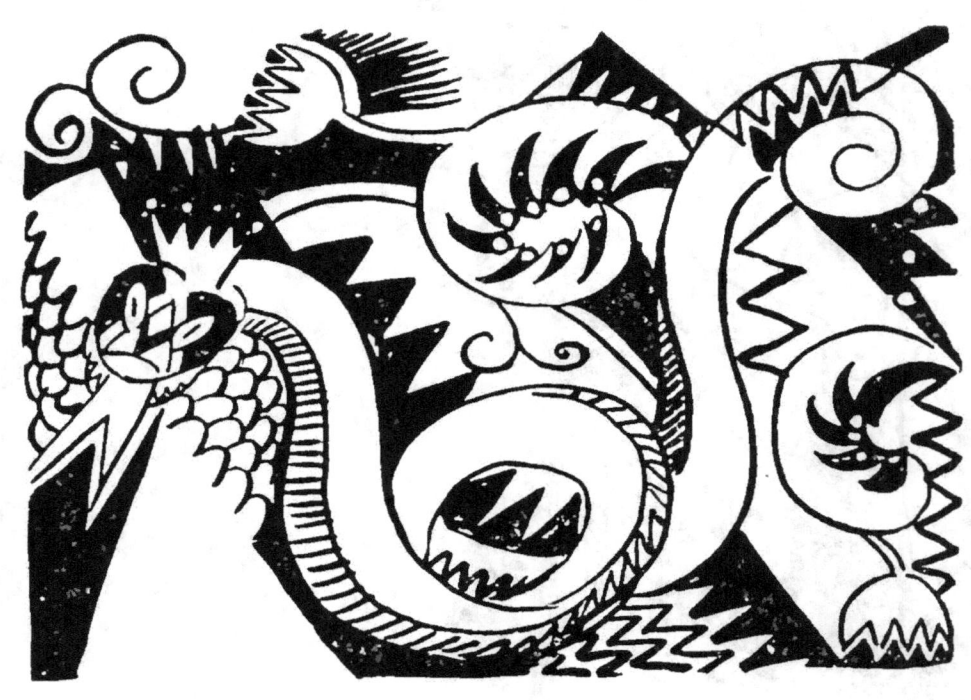

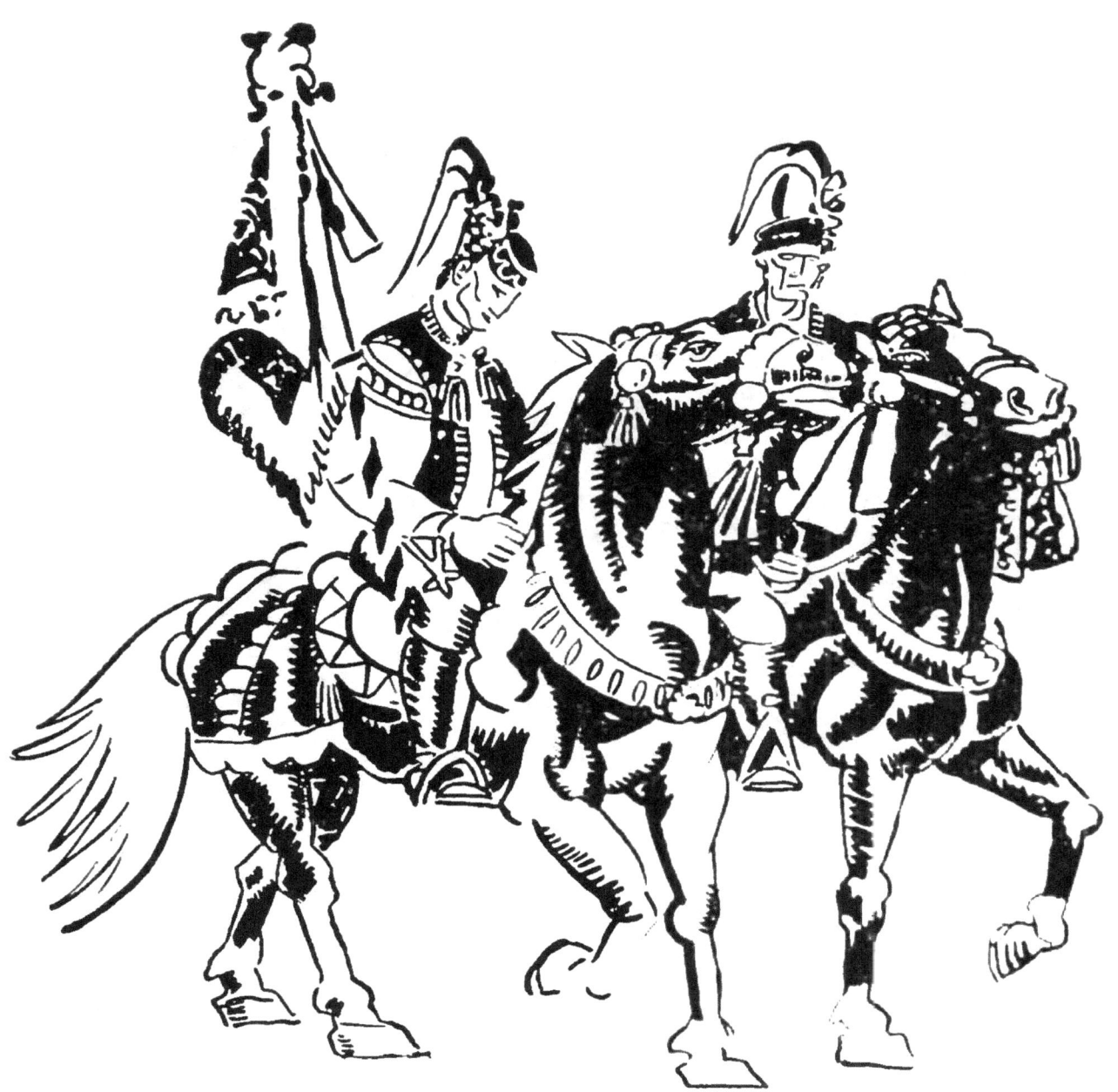

Yirik's horse began to prance and neigh

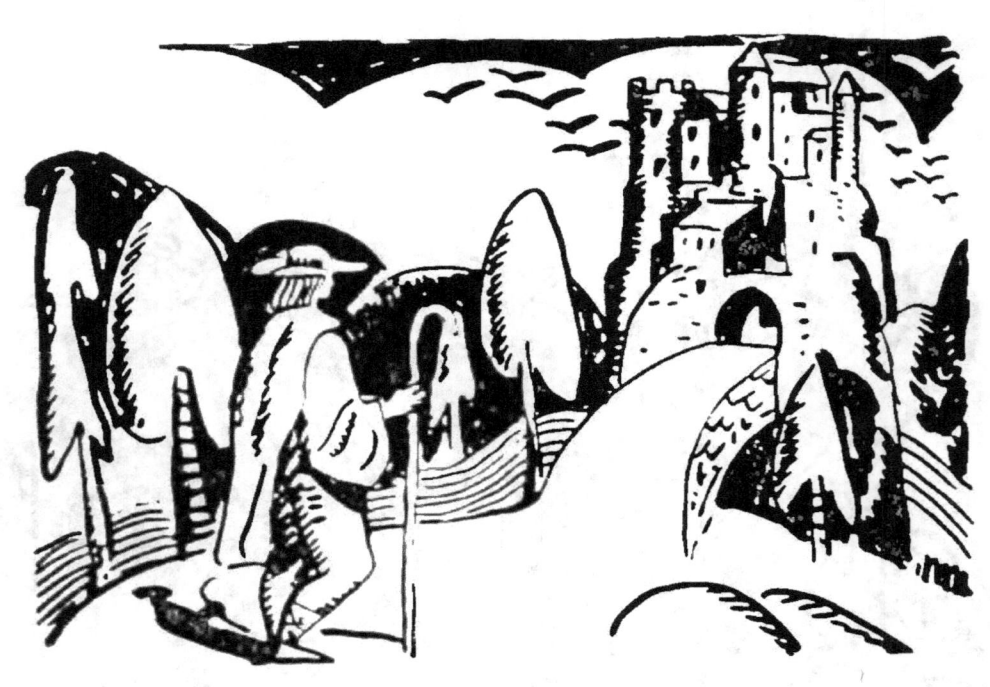

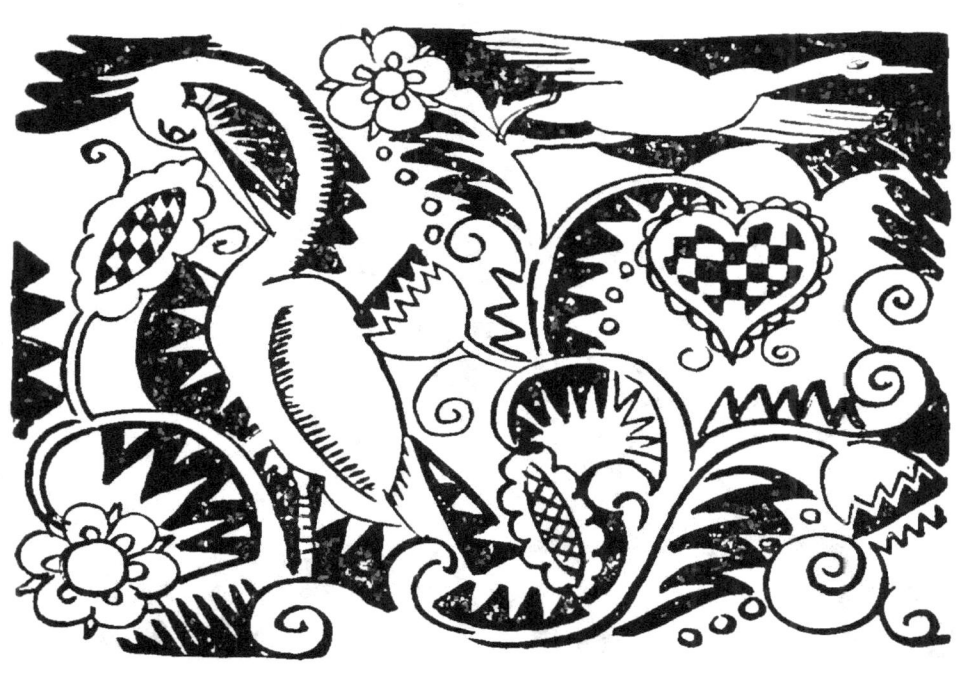

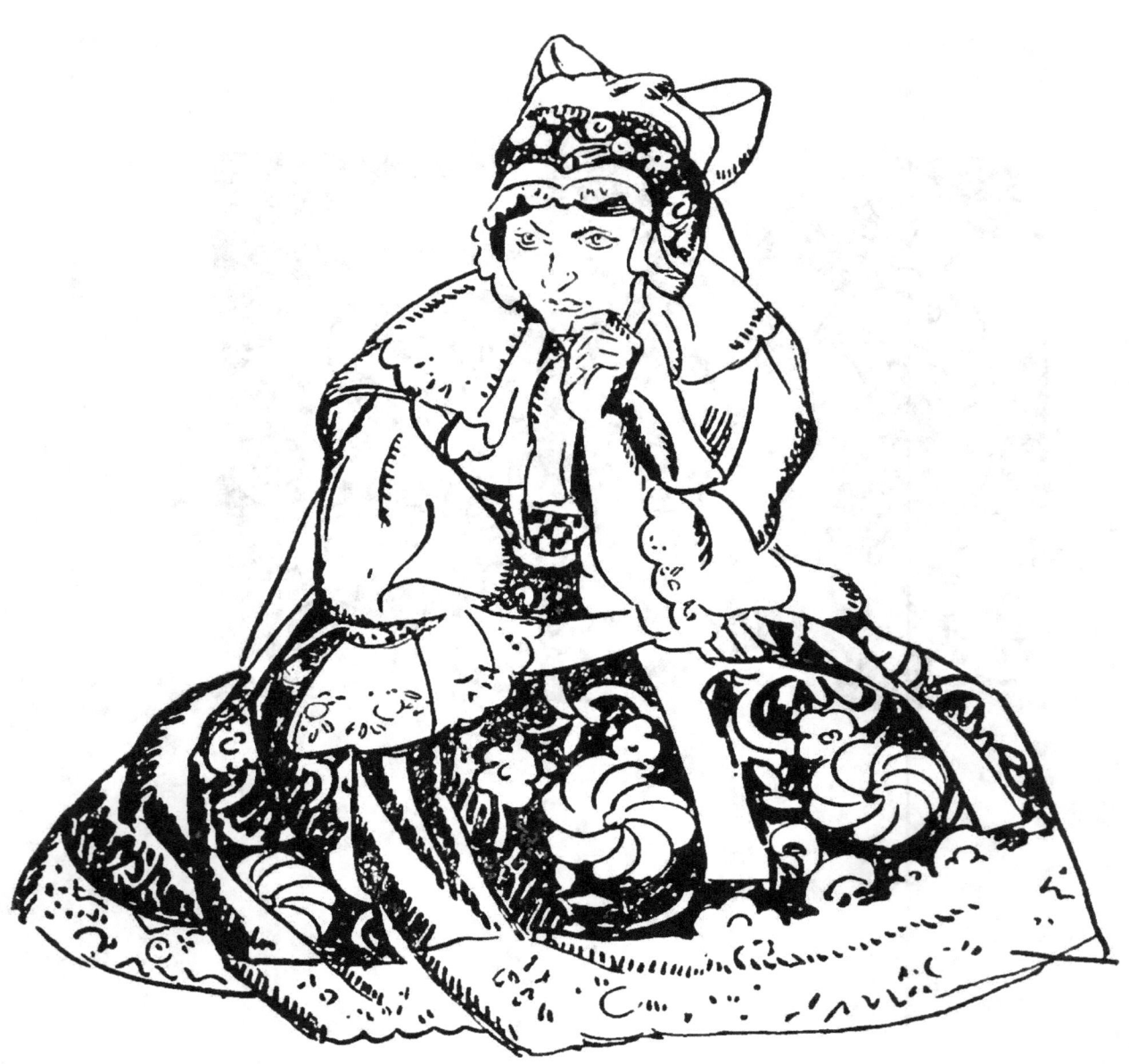

Nedyelka tells Vitazko what to do

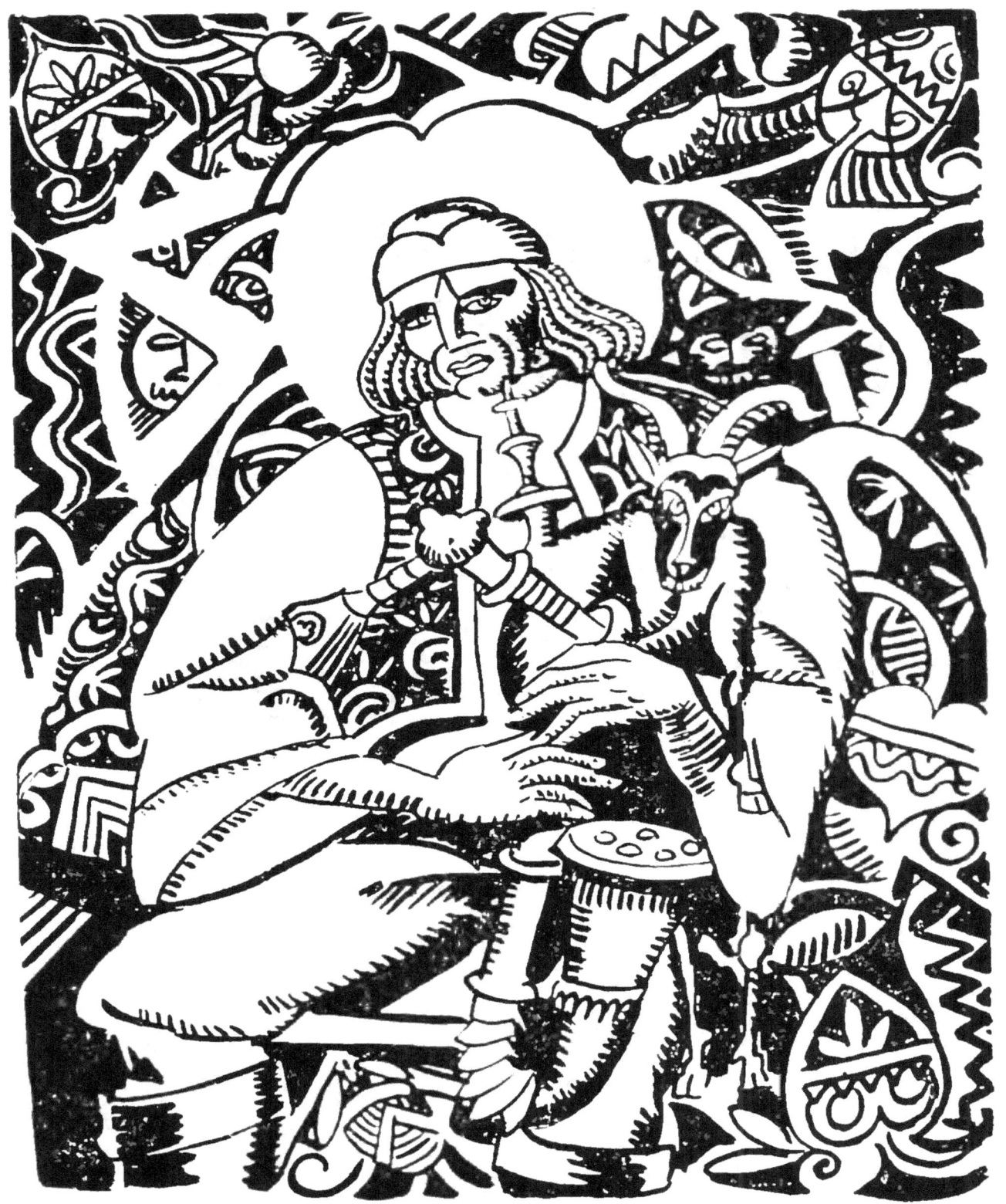

Vitazko disguised as an old village piper

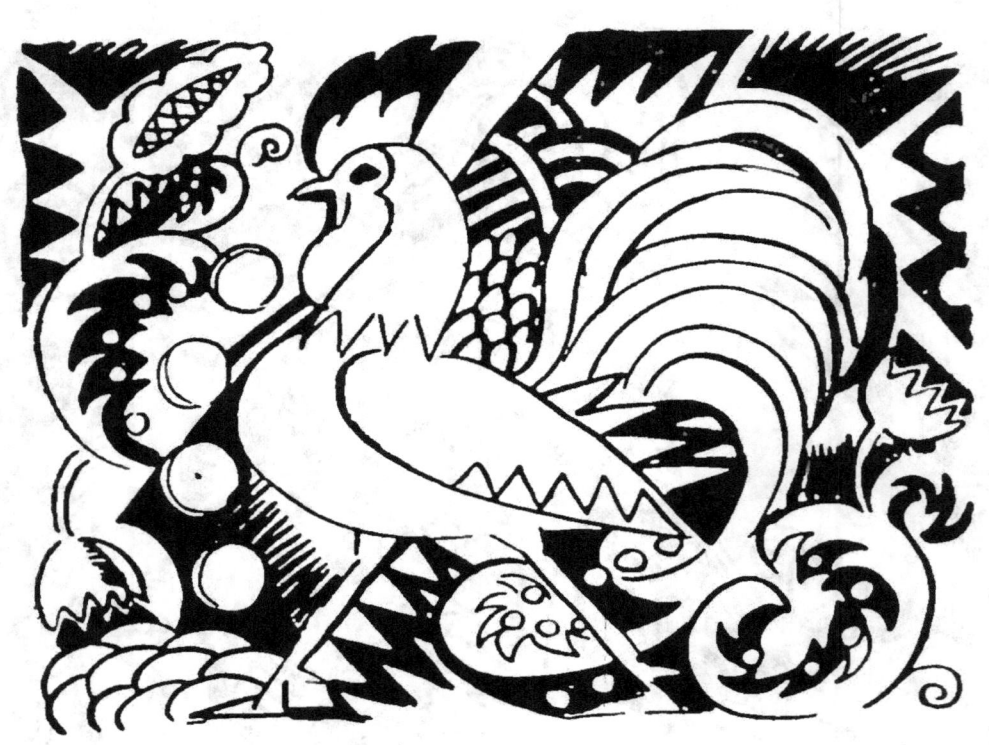

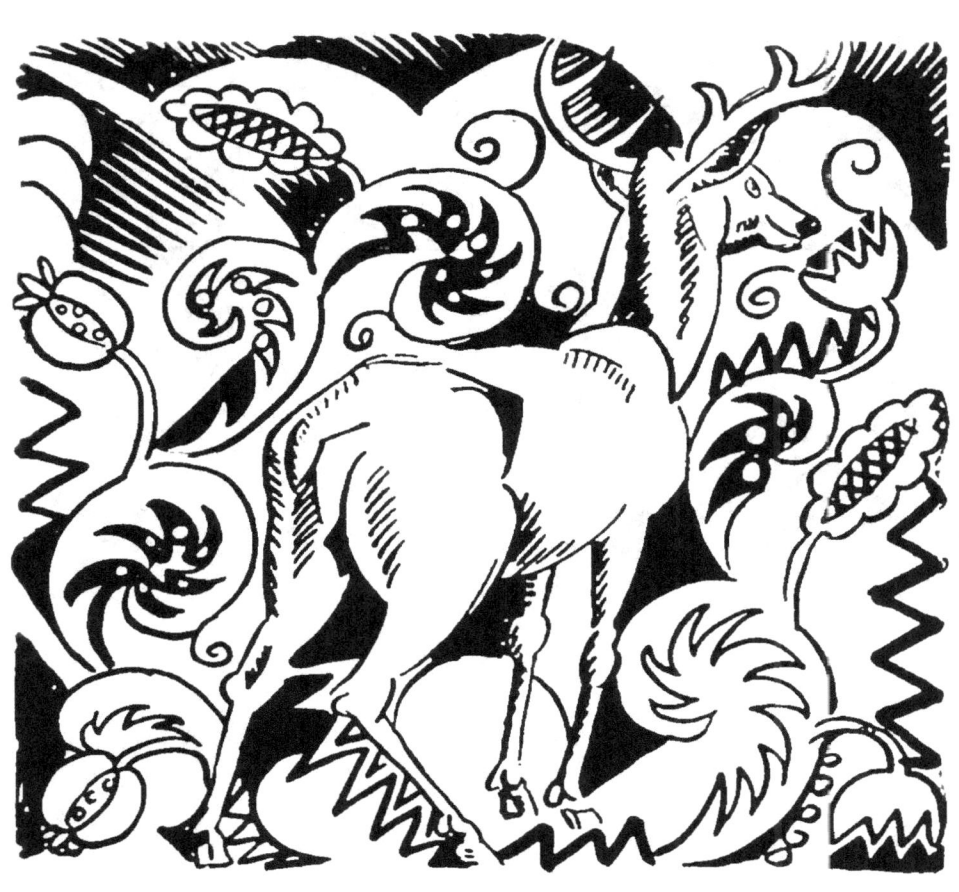

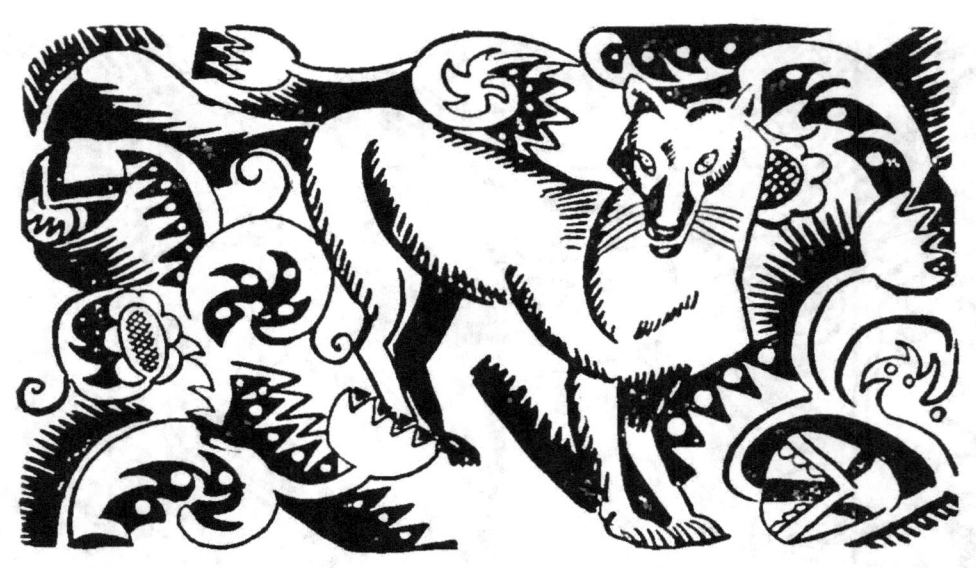

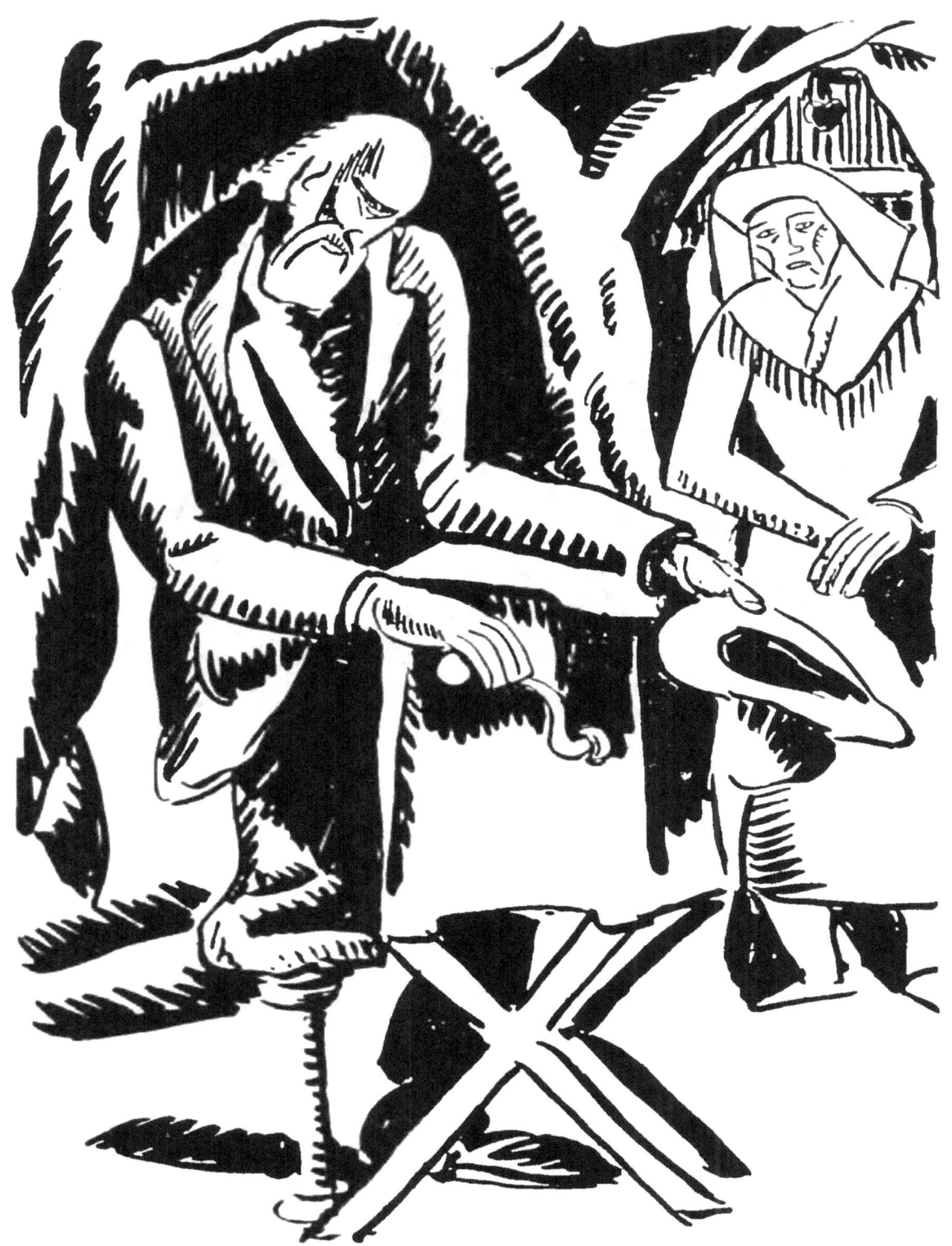

An organ-grinder began playing in front of Granny's cottage

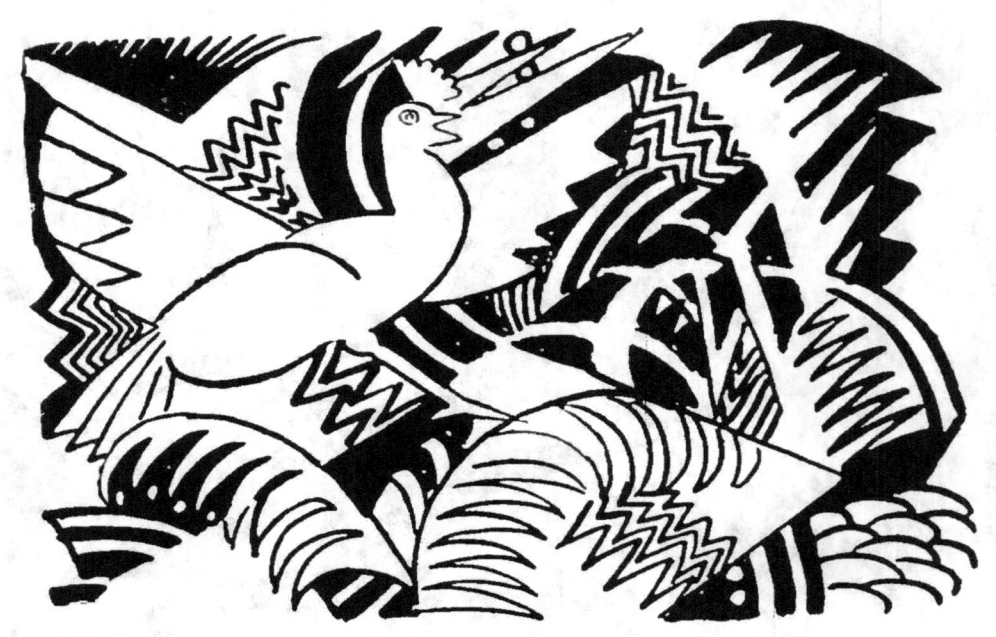

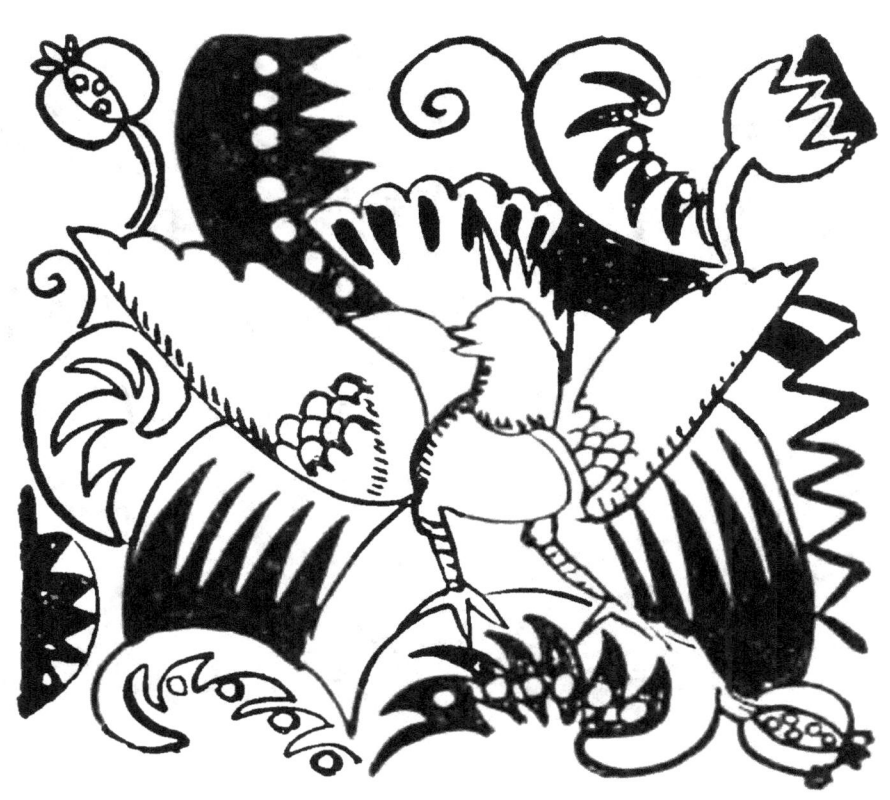

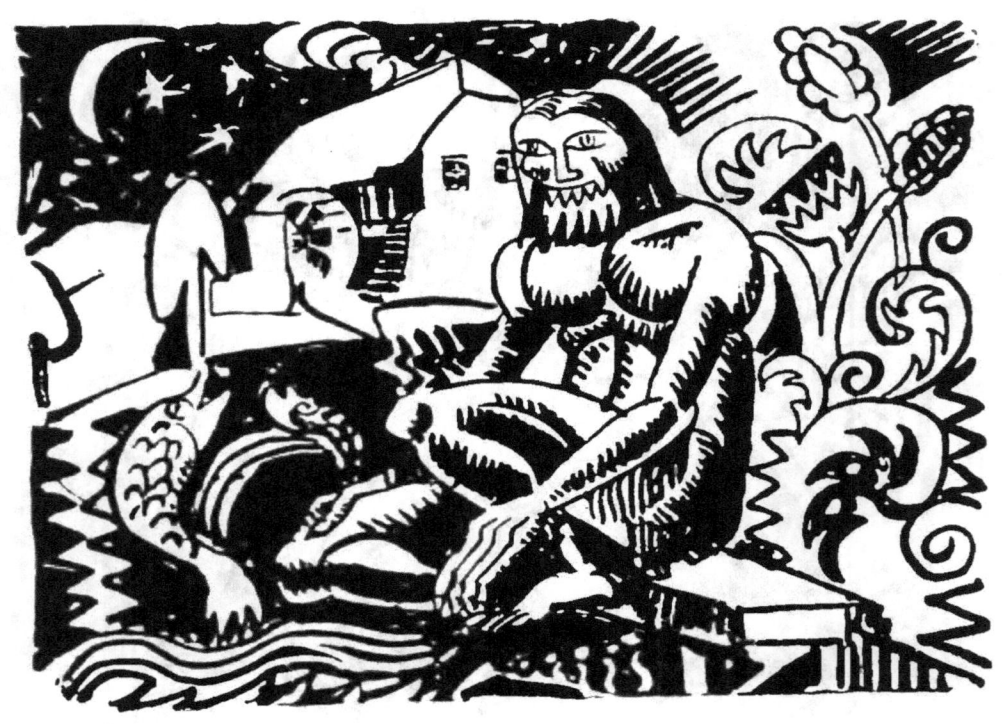

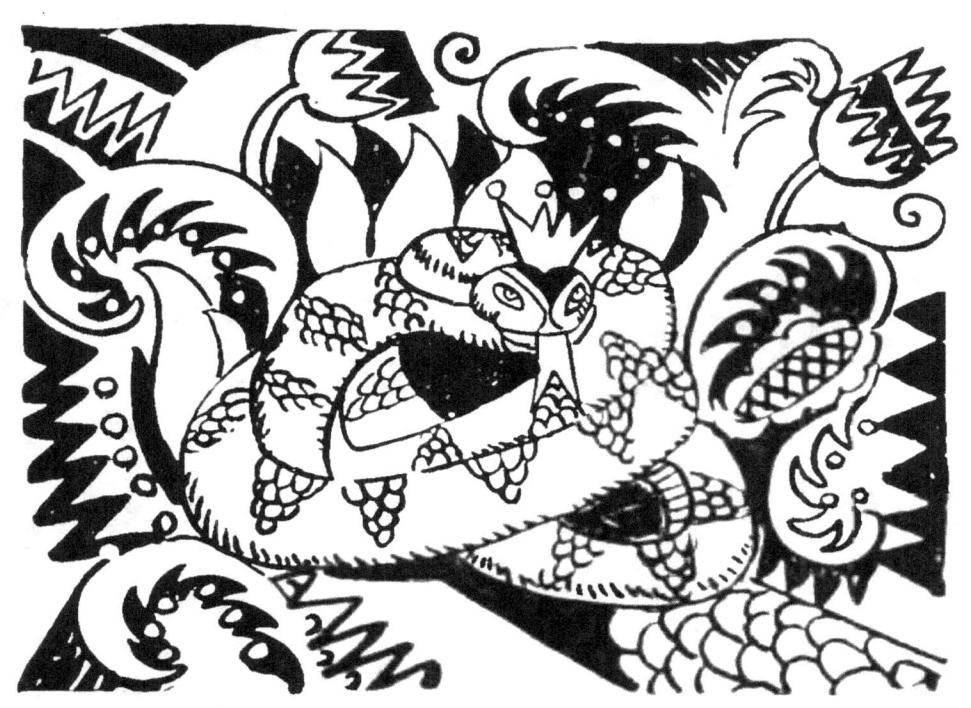

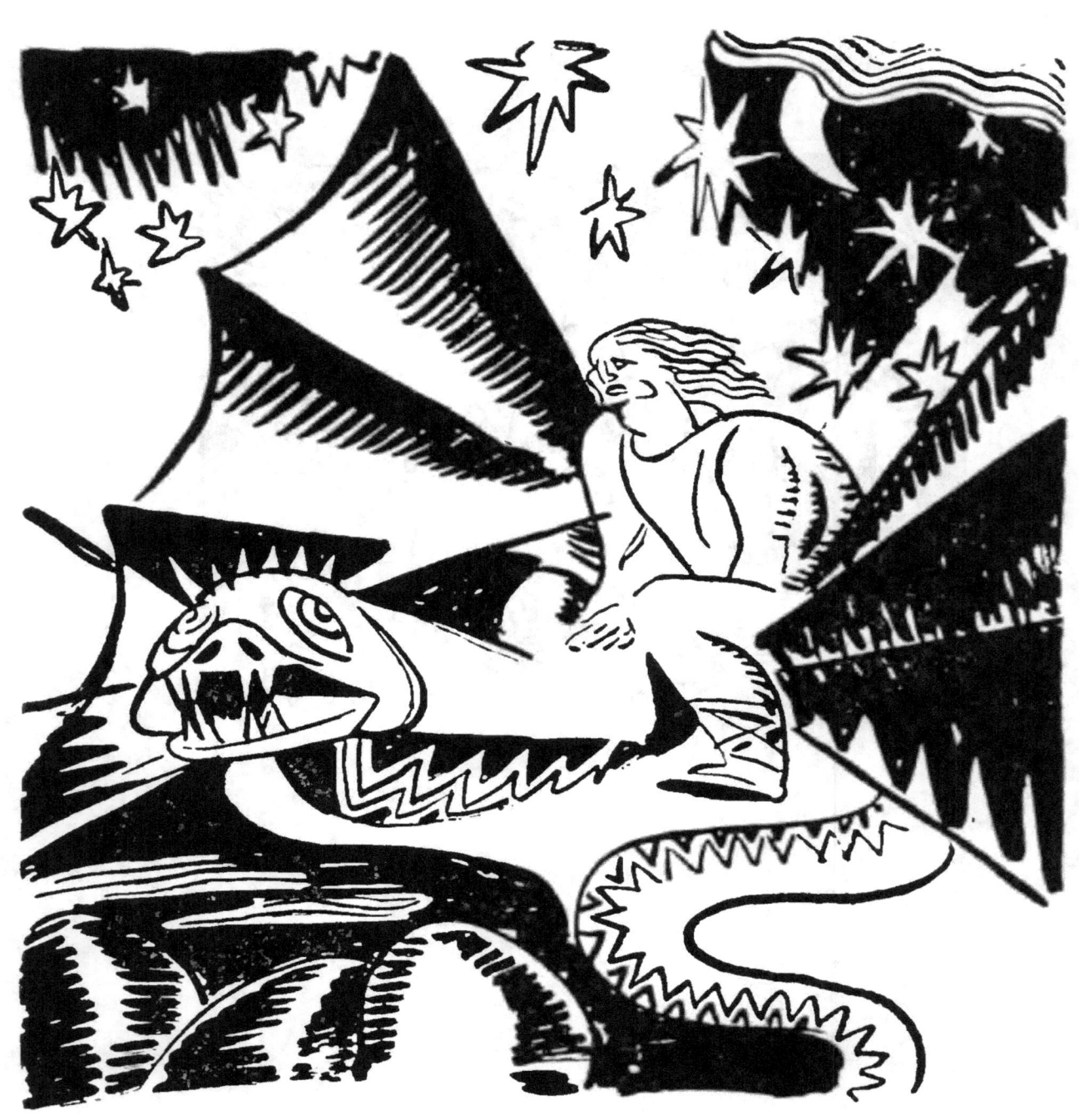

On, on, they went, whizzing through the stars of heaven

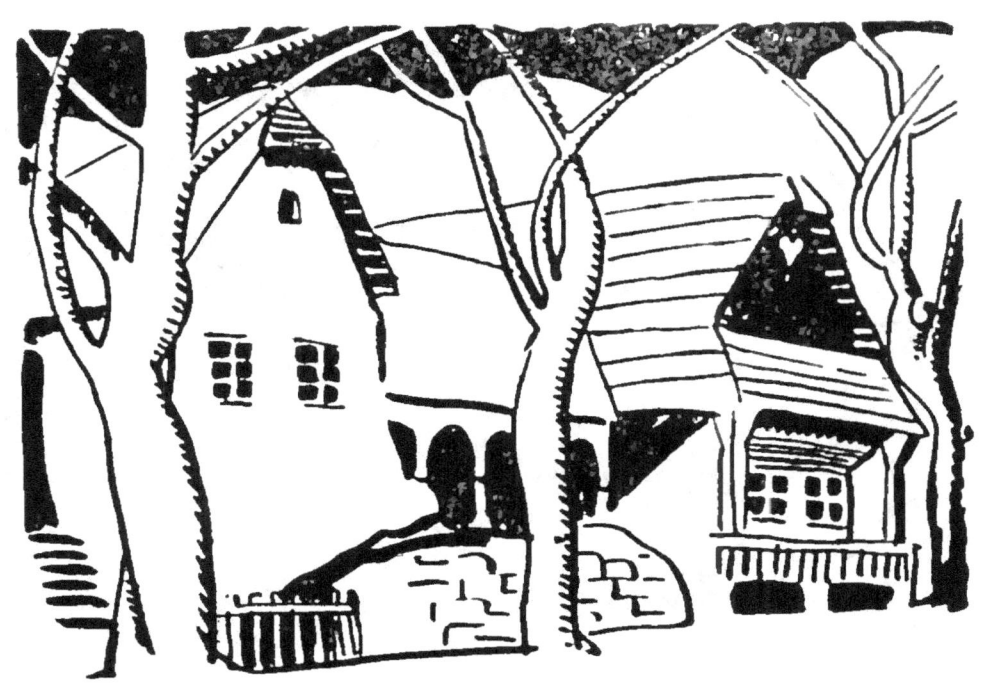

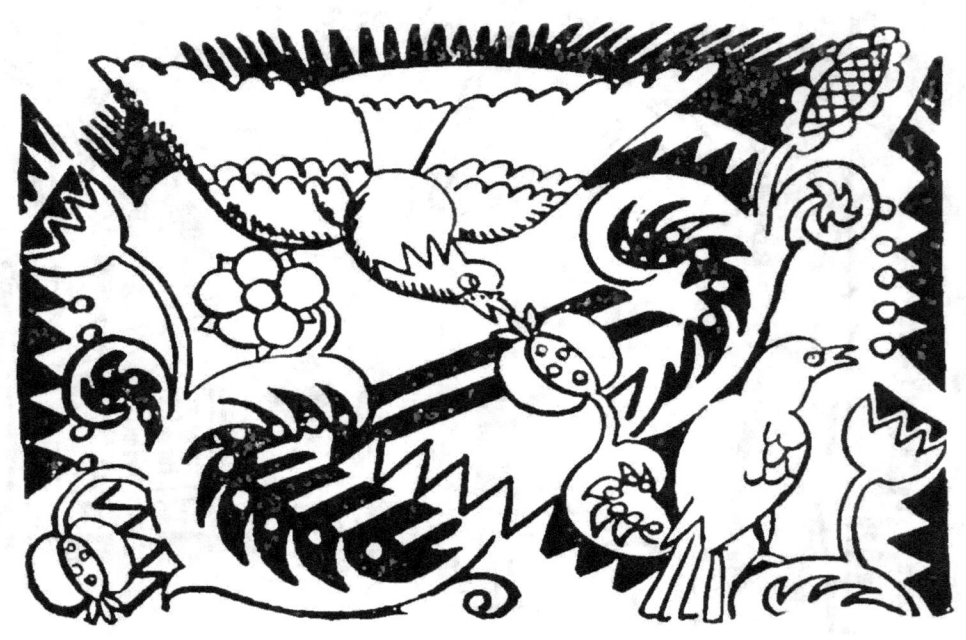

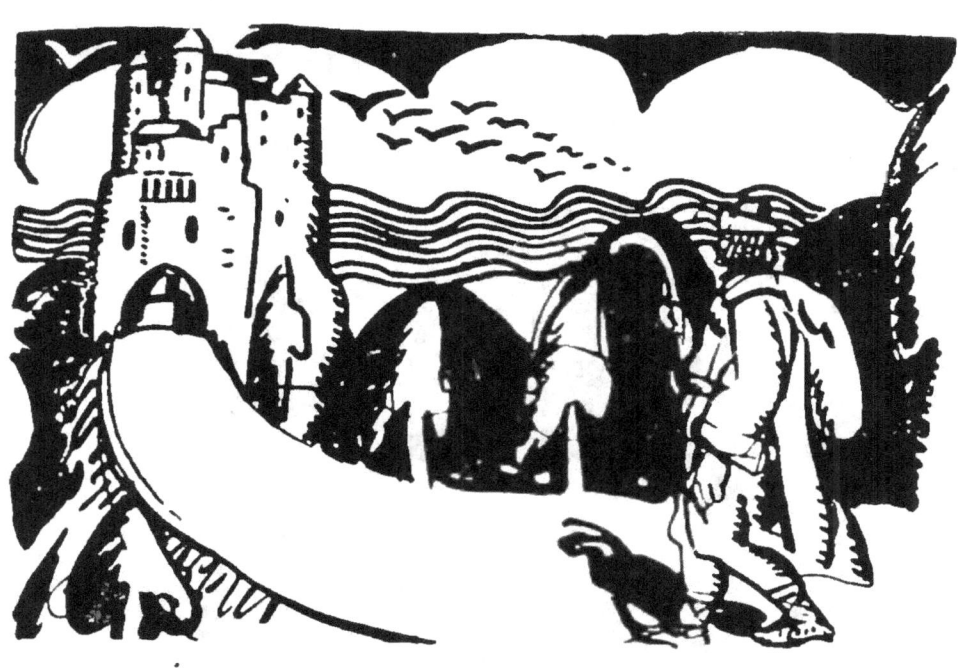

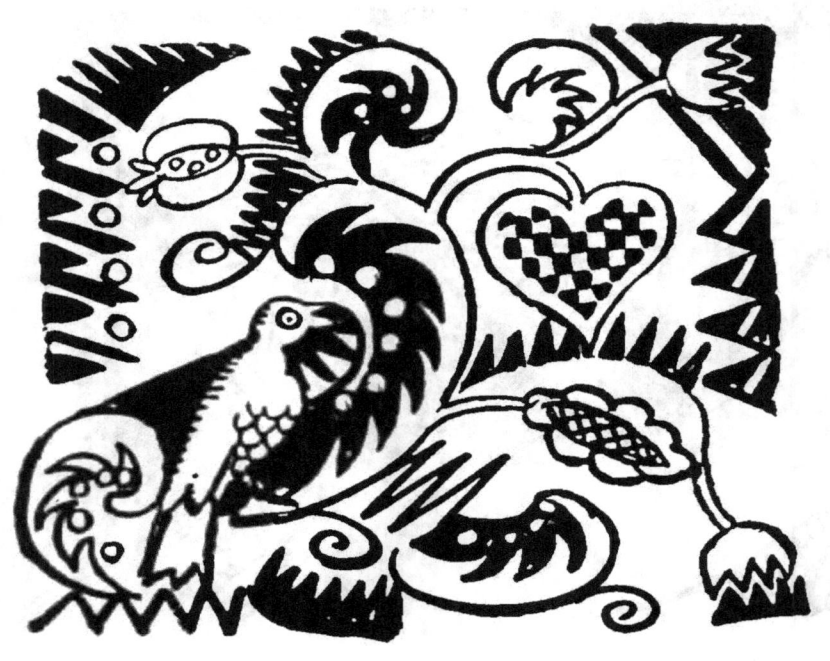

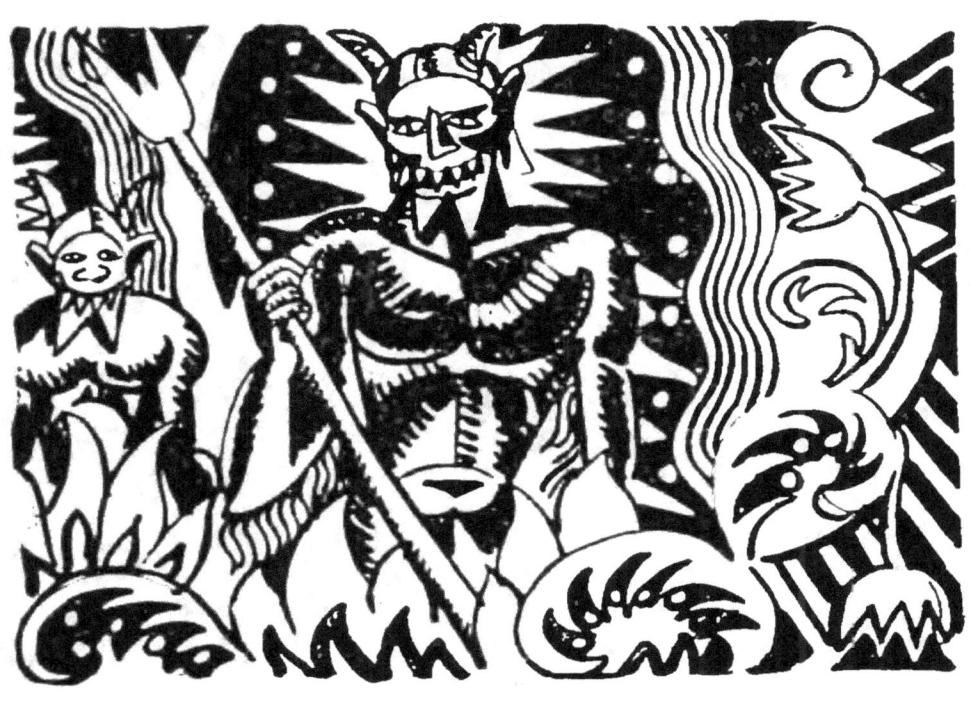

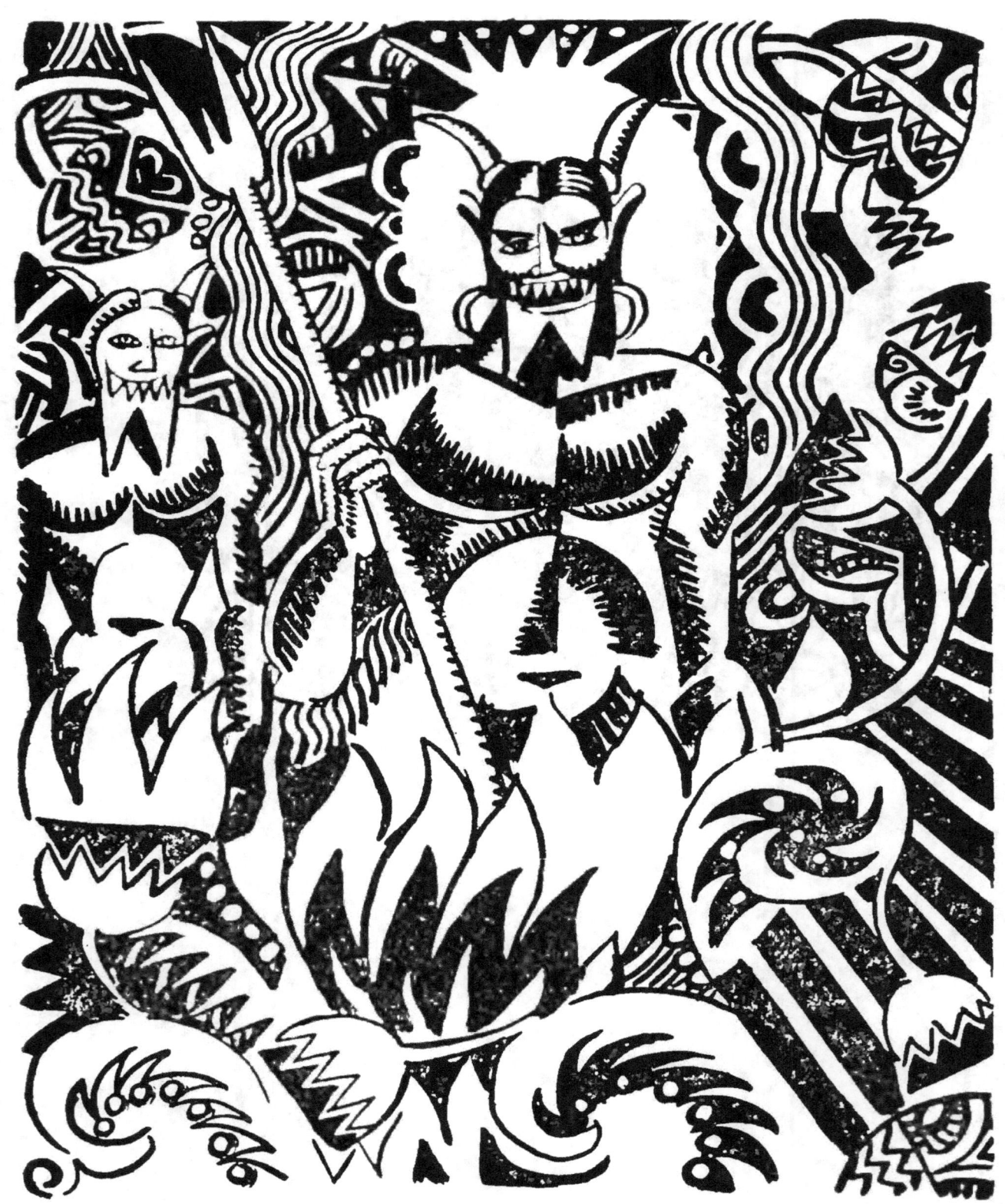

He led them to Prince Lucifer

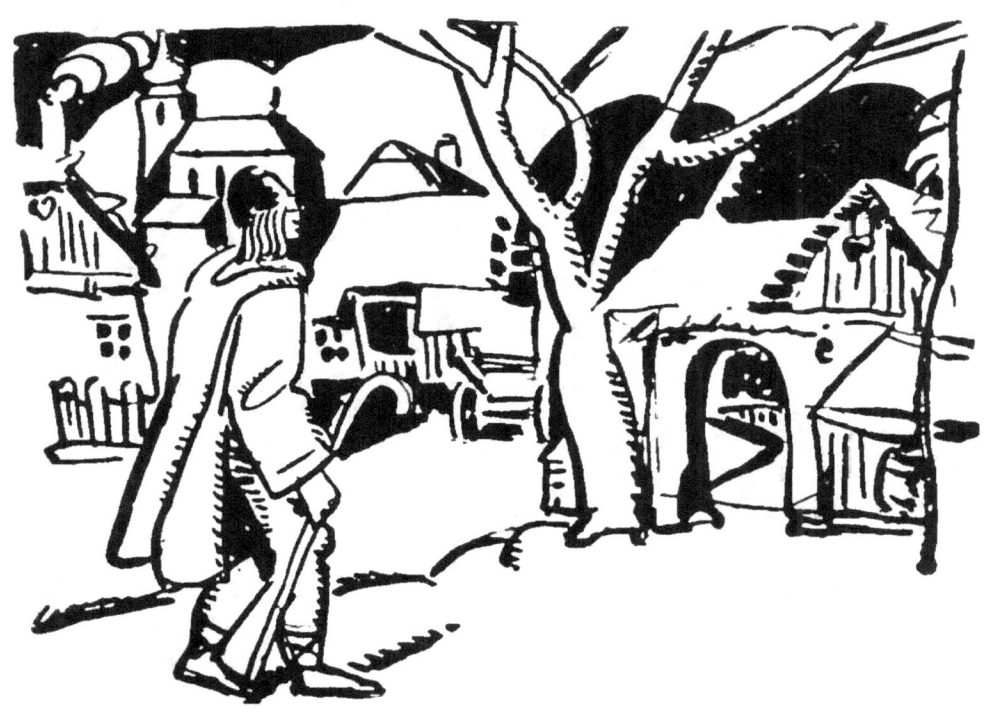

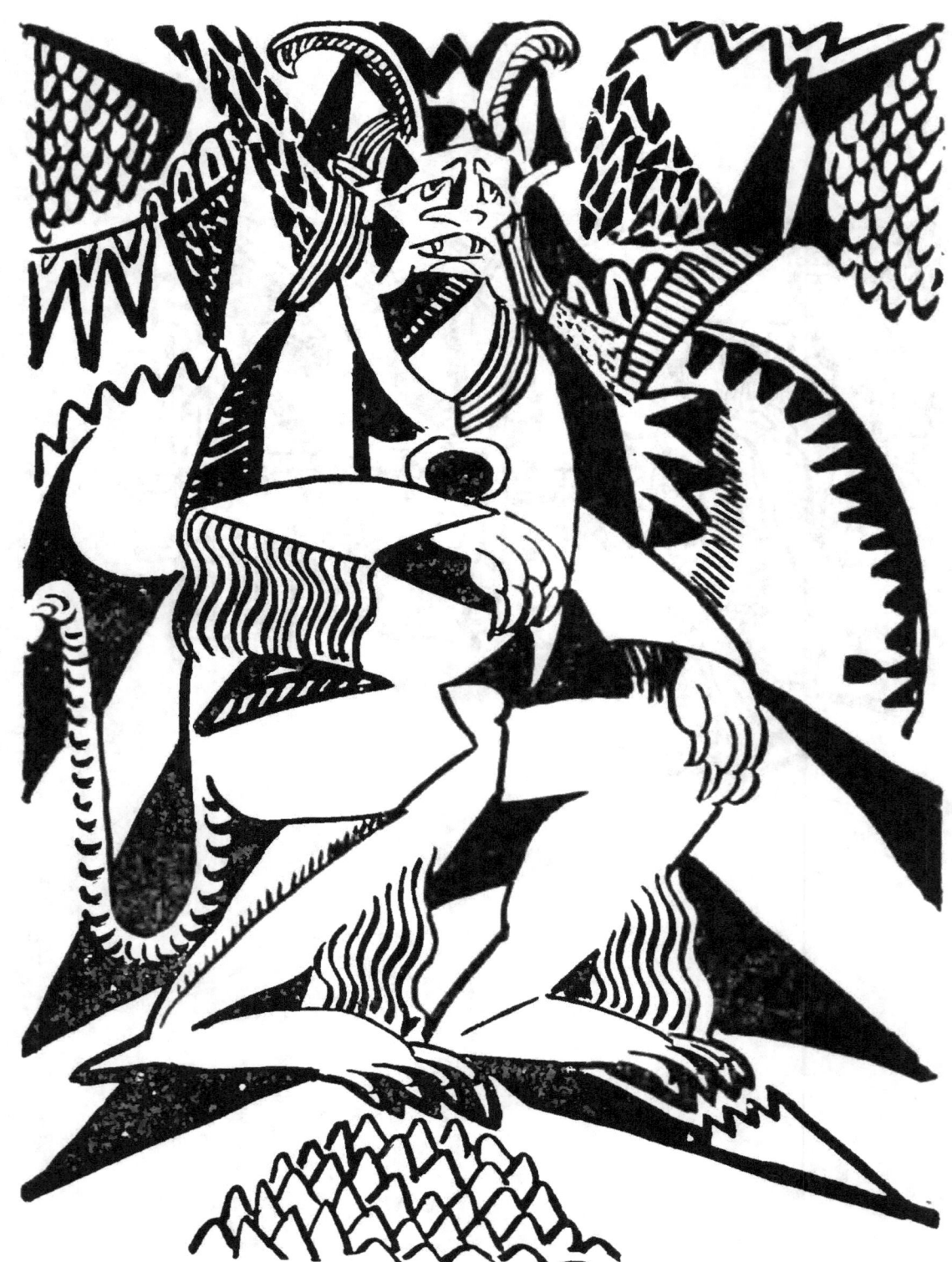

Soon he began to cry.

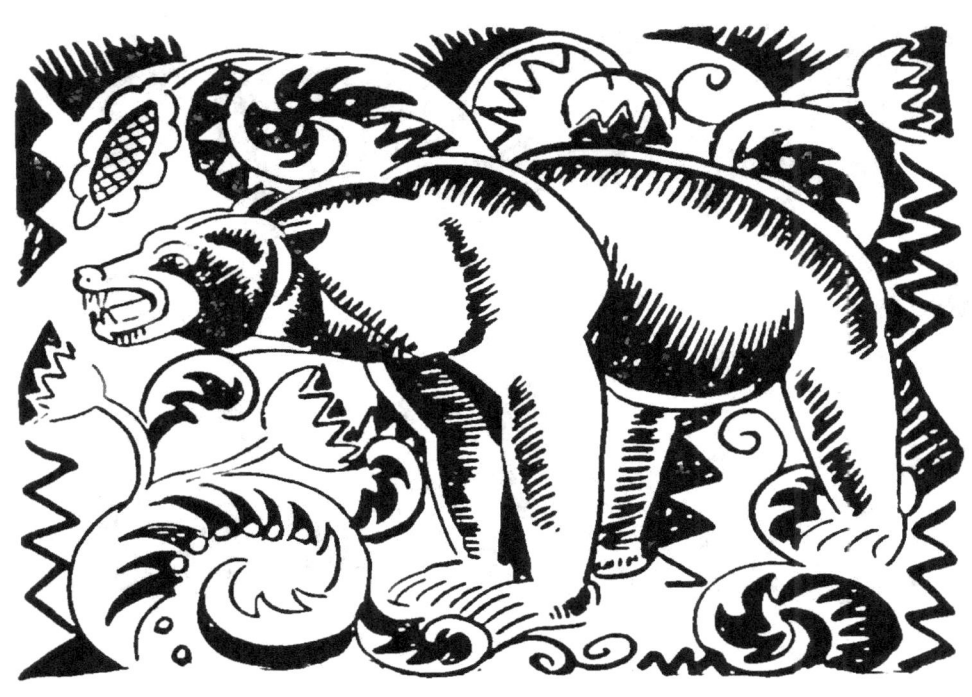

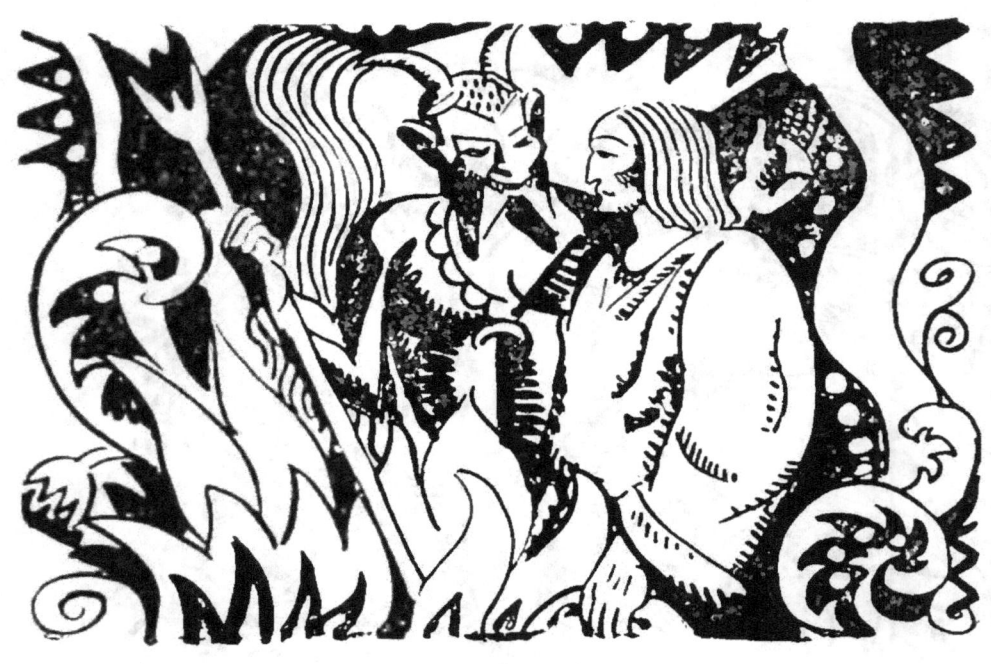

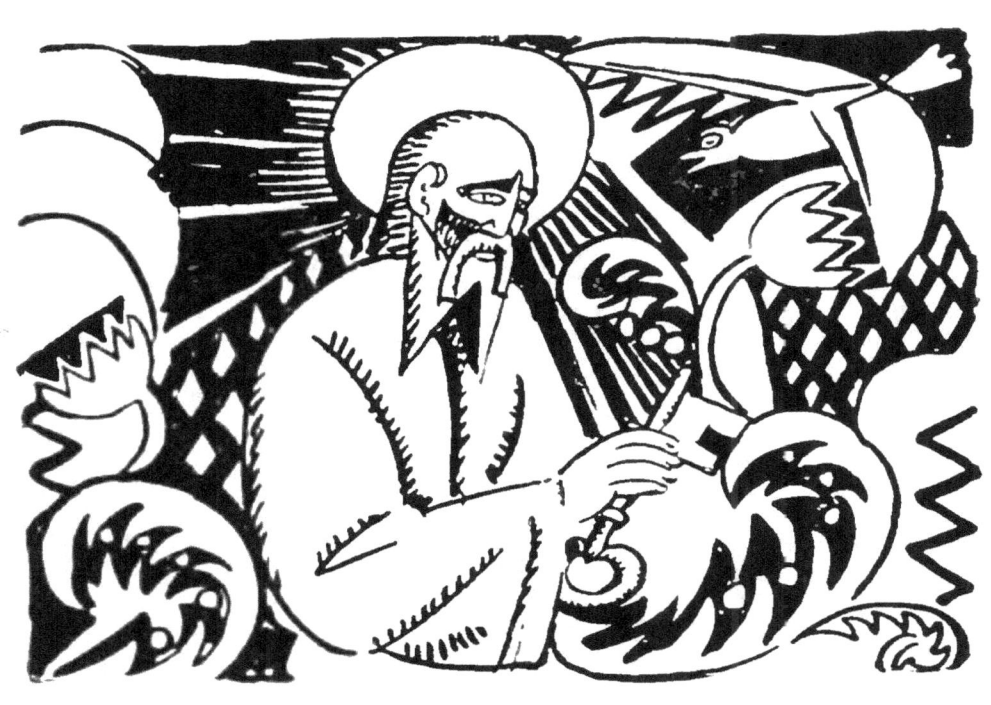